IT WAS ALL A
DREAM

If You Can Dream It, You Can Make It Happen.
We Did!

Yet Dreaming
Damon

IT WAS ALL A DREAM

If You Can Dream It, You Can Make It Happen.
We Did!

SUCCESS

POSSIBILITIES

Brencleveton Donta Truss, Ed.D, Ramone Harper, Bryant Spencer,
Marc P. Desgraves IV, CPA, Tyrish Garrett, Terrence Hall, Terrance Turner, CPA,
Anthony Lewis Ph.D., Herman Moncrief, CPA,
Jeremy Spratling, Demetrice Jones

Contributed By
TDI, Inc.

ISBN: 978-0997431803

TABLE OF CONTENTS

ENDORSEMENTS

"It Was All a Dream hits the awareness, struggles, hopes and triumphs behind the conversations ... the real talk ... that we must continue to have about what inspires our young men, and the role of the HBCU in that inspiration. What do our young men need to know and embrace the greatness within themselves? The answer in part lies in our beloved HBCU higher education community and the power within the culture of these national gems ... shout out to 'Bama State! This group of 11 brothers and ASU alums are walking the walk par excellence... an example of that inspiration. It Was All a Dream is a must read and fresh, uplifting addition to the conversation."

Karyn Scissum Gunn, Ph.D.
Associate Provost for Academic Affairs and
Professor of Microbiology
Alabama State University

Any young person interested in overcoming adversities and dreaming big dreams should unequivocally associate with the men of TDI as described in this book. For over 20 years I have witnessed the maturation of this group of men into productive contributors to society. They are a glowing example of the power of prayer and persistence in the lives of young African American males.

Vergil Chames, III
Former Student Affairs Administrator, Alabama State University
Venture Capitalist, River Region Capital

IT WAS ALL A DREAM is a wonderful book about 11 men who dreamed outside of themselves while on the campus of one of America's greatest historically black colleges, Alabama State University. As an alumna of ASU, I saw the tenacious spirit firsthand from many of these young men. It was just as evident then that they wanted to help and inspire the younger generation to greatness. This is a great read for all future leaders and serves as a great example of what Alabama State University and other historical black colleges or universities can produce. I salute "TallaDallas" in all of their endeavors.

Judge Shera Grant
District Court Judge
Alabama State University, Class of 1999

For the past 20 years I had the opportunity to help provide access to thousands of students looking to gain access to higher education and improve their lives. During this time I had the opportunity to help students in foster care looking for a way out and others who had attended some of the most prestigious private schools on their way to the Ivy League. No matter what the background of the students, they all have one common characteristic: How to reach THAT next level. This book serves as more than motivation to get through college, but a guide through the uncertain road of adulthood through the eyes of 11 men who have experienced many of the peaks and valleys of life on the way to achieving their individual dreams. Through their experiences and friendship the men of TDI have created a tool that can serve as an inspiration to us all to aid in reaching our full potential.

Timothy L. Fields
Associate Dean, Emory University
Morehouse College, Class of 1998

Young African American males are suffering from lack of guidance in the community. It is important that we mentor and show our youth that there is more to life than the streets. Mentorship molded me into the man I am today. Without it I would still have doubts about what I can accomplish. The guidance I had as a youth opened my eyes to something far bigger than myself; they taught me not to be a cancer to society but be a contributor to it. That is why organizations like TDI are important.

Joey Scott
Olympic Developmental Coach
Three-time Olympic Track and Field Coach,
Four-time World Championships Coach

To young brothers with dreams of moving upward and onward toward the illuminating light of intrinsic progress and a raised existence, this book is expressly dedicated! I speak from a biblical sincerity when I say that what you read here from, TDI, is truly what you get! For more than 20 years I, too, have been awestruck by their commitment of spirit, deeplyrooted convictions and this experiential road map that has the power to transform lives. Thank you, TDI–deeply from the souls of our ancestors for accepting the mantle of "each one, reach one" to offer this treasure of hope for one of our greatest community resources...our Black Princes!
To this great endeavor I say, "Ase` my prolific brothers.....Ase`!

Javon D. Brooks, M.S. Ed.
Assistant Superintendent,
Cyber Education Center District
Redford, MI

FOREWORD

There are 107 historically black colleges and universities (HBCUs) in the United States, including public and private institutions, community and four-year institutions, medical and law schools. Even though the historical intent was to provide higher education opportunities for African Americans who could not afford to attend the most affluent state schools, most HBCUs were not and have not been given a sufficient amount of state dollars to keep these schools funded year to year. That's the bad news. The good news is HBCUs' much like the people they serve, find a way to survive and educate their alumni at a very high prestigious standard.

Which leads me to It WAS ALL A DREAM, written by the men of TDI (Turning Dreams Into Realities). This is a book by men who are the product of Alabama State University, an HBCU that framed their individual personalities as well as developed a long-term friendship that ultimately created a nonprofit business built on developing young men and women all across the country. A common theme with all of the personal narratives is the men's personal desires to be great, a greatness that comes from the ability to navigate adverse situations to a point of long-term success.

Greatness and pain are often inseparable. Every time those adverse moments are described from one chapter to another, each author reminds us that we waste our mistakes and disappointments when we fail to learn from them. When we lose sight of our goals and vision, we miss the opportunity to change, grow, and move forward into an increased "Greatness" capacity.

Johnny Stephens
Grassroots Consulting LLC, CEO

INTRODUCTION

Before the year even began, 1972 promised to be momentous. Because it was a leap year, two leap seconds were added to the year, making it 366 days, the longest year in modern history—something that has not been repeated since. The year also yielded groundbreaking highs as well as controversial lows.

President Richard Nixon ordered the development of a space shuttle program. However, in June 1972, there was a break-in at the Democratic National Committee headquarters in Washington, DC—later known as the Watergate scandal—which resulted in a government cover-up and led to Nixon's disgrace and to his resignation two years later. The last draft lottery was held in 1972, a watershed moment in the wind-down of military conscription in the United States during the Vietnam War era; and political activist, scholar, and author Angela Davis was released from jail and later found not guilty of murder.

The first installment of the *Godfather* trilogy was released in theaters, and HBO (Home Box Office) was launched as the longest continuously operating pay television service in the country. To end the year, Gene Cernan, Ronald Evans, and Harrison Schmitt participated in the last manned moon mission to date aboard the *Apollo 17* spacecraft.

That same year, Christopher Wallace—later known as Biggie Smalls, "the King of New York"—was born in Brooklyn, New

York, in the Bedford-Stuyvesant neighborhood. Although he started out as a small-time drug dealer, he would one day become one of the greatest rappers in music history. According to his classic hit "Juicy," he went from negative to positive, changed from a common thief to a successful entertainer, broke the stereotypes of what black men could aspire to be, and learned to live life without fear. Smalls credited all his success to his ability to dream. His lyrics inspired our own dreams.

This book is our story, a chronicle of the lives of 11 African American men from the South who had dreams of becoming successful and changing the way we were perceived because of the color of our skin. Now we are focused on giving back to young people all over the country through our nonprofit organization, Turning Dreams Into Realities, Inc. (TDI).

We share an appreciation for education, relationships, partying, family, success, music, and most importantly a dedication to our dreams. What is the key to our success? Our D.R.E.A.M.S. (Dedication, Relationships, Execution, Attitude, Motivation, and Sacrifice).

We invite you to join us in helping to transform the dreams of other young African American college students through scholarships, mentoring, and professional development by making a tax-deductible contribution. Visit us at www.tdi2r.org.

CHAPTER ONE

THE BEGINNING

BRENCLEVETON DONTA TRUSS, Ed.D

As I sit in the pulpit at Liberty Hill Missionary Baptist Church in Phenix City, Alabama, I think about how I got here. After all the outrageously wrong things I have done, how did I go from where I used to be to where I am now? I realize that I am a story that is not yet complete; and the story is filled with good days and bad, but I have more good days than bad days. As I flash back to my past, I begin to recall the many people and events that have pushed me into my destiny.

Many of the people in the Knoxville area of Talladega, Alabama, lived in poverty, whether they knew it or not. During the late sixties early seventies, many didn't have running water at home, not to mention washers and dryers, so they had to go to wash houses—or, as we called them in Talladega, washeterias. It was just such a washeteria that came to mind when I was thinking of my past.

Pretty ninth-grader Brenda Glover was washing clothes at a washeteria with her grandmother Gussie Mae Glover. Gussie Glover had raised Brenda pretty much as her own child. One day, a young handsome man drove by and saw Brenda and her beautiful legs. He was fit and trim and had curly black hair. They were instantly attracted to each other. Clement Truss decided that day that Brenda would be his, so he pursued her relentlessly. Clement worked at Talladega Foundry, a local mill; and he thought he was on top of the world.

Brenda agreed to a date with Clement, and they became a passionate couple in love. While Brenda was ambitious, Clement was a hardheaded rebel who believed in little—but what he did believe in, he stood by it. If Gussie would not allow him to see Brenda, Clement would angrily speed out of her yard, knocking down her mailbox! But although he was a rebel with his own set of rules, he also was very smart and knew how to make amends. Usually, by the next day, he had returned to Gussie's and fixed her mailbox.

Clement soon won Brenda over, and the couple was married. Soon they discovered they were expecting a child. Unfortunately, their relationship was already a little rocky, filled with passionate verbal and sometimes physical fights. They were young and temperamental, and money was tight.

To complicate the couple's woes, they were unhappy living in Talladega, believing that the town just wasn't the right fit for them. Brenda adamantly proclaimed that her child could not be born in Talladega; he had to be born somewhere else. So after much discussion, Clement and Brenda decided they would start their new lives in Atlanta, Georgia. Brenda desperately wanted her child to be born in a place filled with hope and opportunity, so the Trusses headed east.

A Child Is Born

In 1972, Atlanta seemed to be bursting with opportunities, and it quickly became a place of hope for many African Americans. Soon after the Trusses arrived, Brenda gave birth to me, Brencleveton Donta Truss—a baby with a unique name (which came from putting together the names of my mother, Brenda; my father, Clement; and my grandfather, Cleveland). More importantly, Brenda and Clement believed that I would become president of the United States or the CEO of a large company. To them, my name, Brencleveton, sounded presidential, while my middle name, Donta, was added so somebody could pronounce at least part of my name.

I was a peculiar child from a peculiar background. By this time, my parents' marriage was strained by my father's temper and my mother's relentless will. To try to provide a brighter future for our family, Dad enlisted in the Army and left for basic training. Mom, deciding that she did not want to be dependent on anyone while Dad was away, enlisted in the Army, too. Compared to the availability of low-paying jobs at the time, the military offered a much better opportunity, especially for African Americans.

Though joining the Army solved their employment issues, it didn't solve my parents' marital and family problems. Their military duties left them little time to navigate the responsibilities of their young family. Just getting a babysitter for me was a challenge, so they sent me to Talladega to live with my great-grandmother Gussie.

I loved my grandmother and cherished all the time I spent with her. Every night, Grandmother Gussie and I would go to a different church. As a child, that was like having a different adventure every night! I was delighted by the joyful singing and being able to play with the other children. I enjoyed hearing the different hymns and listening to various pastors preach in the country churches we visited.

After four years in the military, my parents returned to Talladega, where they both worked at the Anniston Army Depot. Their new jobs gave them more financial security than they had ever had before, but money was still tight. They moved to a two-bedroom trailer that they purchased in Kentucky on land previously owned by Gussie and her husband, Randle, my great grandfather.

Randle, the patriarch of the Glover family, was a hard-working construction worker who helped build many steam plants and dams in Birmingham, Alabama; raised his children; and took in other children who needed care. His love and kindness and big heart continue to be a big part of the lives of members of the Glover family.

Never one to settle for anything less than the best, my mother demanded that Dad renovate a house they got from Grandfather Randle. Although they had better jobs and a place to live, unfortunately, acquiring the land in Talladega was the beginning of the end for my parents' marriage.

At four years old, I was soon to experience a strange incident that would change the course of my life. My rambunctious cousin, four-year-old Katrina, and I decided to play with the keys to our grandmother's new car. However, playing with the keys led to us starting the car and trying to drive! We blamed each other, but I'm the one—daring Donta—who concocted the plan to take the car for a joyride. We ended up ramming the car into our aunt's trailer before Katrina jumped out of the car.

After leaping from the car, she was run over but miraculously was unhurt. God was already watching over me.

After our dangerous first turn at the wheel, I got the first beat-down I can remember. Soon, I found myself in an all-white preschool so I could try to focus all of those persuasive and creative skills toward something good and not mischievous.

A Love for Education (and the Ladies)

When I started school, I realized that I had a few talents that could not be ignored: I loved reading, and I loved girls. Reading became my way out of all the trouble I got into. In elementary school, I was placed in an advanced reading class that included the best and the brightest students. This was the most amazing class I had ever been in.

I developed my love of reading during the rockiest times of my parents' marriage. When they argued, I would read one of our family encyclopedias. Before the Internet, encyclopedias held a special place of honor in most homes, especially in those of African Americans. I read these books from cover to cover, which made me believe I could learn and understand anything.

My love for girls coincided with my concern with my image and how others perceived me. I was athletic—or at least I thought so—and I had dimples that everyone seemed to love. I worked my athleticism and those dimples to the max, although both would later land me in trouble.

First crushes can be brutal, and my first crush was no exception. I liked the smartest and cutest little girl I had ever known, May Wilson. She was my all in all! However, she would never be my girlfriend, and I was better because of it. She made me work hard chasing her and showed me that I could be turned down.

While still in elementary school, I met a teacher who ended up becoming part of my family: Mrs. Georgia Goodwine. She was my toughest but best teacher during those years. She not only taught me in school, but she also was my Cub Scout leader. It was amazing that no men stepped up to handle the task, but it didn't matter because she filled the gap. She was great, but it wasn't just Mrs. Goodwine's wisdom and intelligence that kept me in the Scouts. She also had a cute daughter!

During my years in the Cub Scouts, I developed a couple of attributes that would stay with me forever. These attributes were a commitment to complete a task and self-love. Mrs. Goodwine showed us that we must complete the task at hand, and she inspired me to have pride in myself.

I was also inspired by the relationship between Mrs. Goodwine and her son. It was similar to the relationship I had with my mother. Mrs. Goodwine had the type of relationship that challenged her son to be his best, and I always admired their relationship.

My own mother was my rock when I was growing up. She and I were like Batman and Robin because we were always together. She was outspoken and ambitious, so she attended a community college and earned a two-year degree in mental health. She went to school part-time while working a full-time job. She did her internship at a convalescent center, and I was with her the whole time. I am very proud of her academic accomplishments.

My father is one of the hardest-working men I know. I loved him for that. He taught me his work ethic as well as how to be a man. He was respected and feared because of his matter-of-fact attitude. He could also be somewhat mean at times; but I knew that despite that, he had my back. He has always been a gap-filler for me. When I was younger, I was afraid of him. In many ways this was good because I avoided trouble, but it caused me to miss a lot of good years of learning from him because I just wanted to do what he asked and stay out of his way. He was still a good dad.

I often wished my parents had made it! I love them both, but life happens!

By the time I got to middle school, I had found a new love: football. I loved the sport, and I was good at it. I was fast and tough, and I used football to heal the pain from my home life and my parents' rocky relationship. Football taught me many life lessons, including being part of a team and doing my part to ensure the team's success. I even won the MVP award during that time.

My coach, Coach Odell, was an amazing leader, and he played a major role in my life. Sometimes, I think he believed in me more than I believed in myself. He was a football genius who gave up his time to coach some young knuckleheads in the small town of Lincoln, Alabama. He taught us never to give up, and we believed that we could beat anybody. He also instilled in us that practice does make perfect.

It was during my time on the football team that I became close friends with Ryan Dawson and Darrell Pearson. We were ride or die!

They taught me about friendship, and I would have done anything for them. They were committed to being the best in the game.

One day, while hanging out with Ryan and Darrell, I saw a girl named Latina. She was cute but had an edge. If you're from the country, you might have called her "fast." Latina was younger than me, but she was a slick-talker and clearly more experienced than I was. It was my first real love!

In my own middle-school way, I loved Latina. She knew what to say and how to say it, and it didn't hurt that she also knew how to kiss. She was a cheerleader, so I would see her at our football games. We also went on Educational Talent Search trips together. Educational Talent Search is a federally funded program that helped people from low-income homes to go to college and be successful. The program made it possible for us to go on culturally enriching trips.

When I found out Latina was going on a college tour, I quickly registered for the trip. On the day of the trip, I showed up excited and ready to go, but Latina was nowhere to be found. I was so upset!

Without Latina, our group traveled to Alabama State University. At first, I thought I was not going to like the school, but I quickly realized that this was a different world. I was less than 100 miles from home, but I discovered a new world and my future home. The day I arrived on campus, I saw girls wearing their Greek colors: pink and green, red and white, and blue and white. I knew I was in heaven. I had never seen this many black people in my life, and they all looked prosperous!

Then we saw guys dancing. They were dressed in their colors, red and white, and brandished their canes while they danced. Later, I discovered that they were "stepping," or step-dancing, which is popular at many Greek shows. These brothers were as smooth as ice. I knew at that moment I wanted to be just like them. The dream had started!

A Love for God

Growing up, it seems everything in my life was centered around Sycamore Missionary Baptist Church. My best mentors came from that church: Mrs. Christine Gaddis; Mrs. Callie Mae Brock; and Pastor Montgomery, who was also an Alabama State University graduate. It was through these dedicated people that I viewed the world, and they were always around to provide guidance for me along life's path.

During my time at Sycamore, I was in many Christmas plays and Sunday school activities. My mother kept me in church, and I enjoyed being there because there were always girls there; but little did I know that being in church was the beginning of a life-long journey.

God and I went through so many issues along the way—some are too devastating to mention. I found myself in situations where I was certain I was going to lose, but God kept me and allowed me to survive. On many occasions, I told God that if He got me out of a particular situation, I would not do it again. Later, I would find myself right back in that same situation, but God still kept me. I didn't always understand why, but God protected me.

Mentorship

While I was in middle school, my favorite teacher was Mr. Freddie Brown. Mr. Brown was the man, and I wanted to be just like him. I rode in his Nissan 280z when he took me to a science fair competition at Talladega College. I hated science at that time and had the most awful science project to take to the fair, but my consolation prize was to ride in Mr. Brown's car while my friends rode in a van.

Mr. Brown knew about my difficult home life, so he was doing what he could to encourage me. My parents were going through a divorce, and I needed as much positive motivation as I could get. He told me I had potential and said that there was something about me that would take me to the next level. He said that no matter what happened, I should keep pushing forward and never sit still.

Though he was encouraging, Mr. Brown was also tough on me, accepted no excuses, and challenged me mentally. Not only did he teach me to express myself verbally, he also sharpened my reasoning skills by questioning my rationale. He inspired me to be the best.

Even his car motivated me. I wanted to be able to afford a car like Mr. Brown, and I knew I had to work hard to do it. He was an amazing blessing in my life because he gave back when he didn't have to. He taught me the power of mentorship and how important it is to be excellent. For those reasons, Mr. Brown became a superstar in my life.

Lesson Learned

Freshman year at Talladega High, I was the man! I had a whole world of opportunities in front of me. Unfortunately, I didn't always make the best choices. I had a chance to choose an advanced degree, but because of peer pressure I decided not to enter the advanced degree program. This would prove to be the first of many mistakes I made during my time in high school. Looking back, it seems as if I was determined to sabotage any chances for success I might have had.

It's hard to believe that students were asked to make such weighty decisions at such a young age. Many students were coming from backgrounds where even their parents weren't equipped to make such decisions for their children. Most parents believed that if their children chose the advanced degree program and their GPAs were low, that would cause them not to graduate with their class. So students were encouraged, many by their families, to avoid the honors program. Fortunately for me, I still took many of the classes I needed for college.

Though I didn't shoot for the stars with the advanced degree program, I still did well, and my high school years were filled with drama and fun. Most of my troubles related to my curfew, though. My mother demanded that I be home around 11:00 P.M. I hated curfew. In fact, during my senior year, my mother and I argued about my curfew. (My real motivation for a later curfew involved my girlfriend, who could stay out until 1:00 A.M.) I took a stand and told her that if she didn't allow me a more generous curfew, I would not go to school.

After my tantrum, my spitfire of a mother was as angry as I'd ever seen her. She ordered me to get in the car, and we drove to the Talladega police station. Before I knew it, I was behind bars and talking to the biggest, meanest criminal I had ever seen!

> Sometimes you have to fight like hell to make your point and achieve your goal.

This man told me about how bad it was in jail and how I didn't want to end up as his girlfriend. I was scared to death! He also mentioned that because he didn't get an education, it cost him many opportunities.

As scared as I was, I was also thinking that my mother had lost her mind. I didn't think I had done anything to make her put me in jail with this maniac of a criminal. However, I realized at that moment what it would mean to my mother for me to graduate from school. She had taken a stand in life for me, and she was not going to allow me to mess up my chance to get an education.

I left that jail a different person. From that point on, I made sure I was home by 11:00—well before my curfew. That day, my mother taught me that drastic situations call for drastic measures. Sometimes you have to fight like hell to make your point and achieve your goal. She wanted to show me what could happen to me if I didn't get my diploma; and her goal was to get me through school and show my father that even though they were divorced, her only child was going to make it, no matter what happened. She would tell anyone that I was going to make it some way, somehow!

However, even my mother's best efforts didn't stop all of the life-changing things that would happen to me. One day, I was summoned to my girlfriend's sister's house. I knew the meeting was serious when I saw the look in my girlfriend's eyes.

At 19, I was getting ready to start college, but I was also going to be a father. My timing couldn't have been any worse. I had dreams for my future, and now I thought my life was over even before it began. What I didn't know was that the beginning of a life would ultimately change my life.

Soon, I welcomed into the world my daughter, Kayla Donielle. Her arrival forced me to grow up quickly. I would have to work all during my college years, but it was the best thing for me. Her birth taught me responsibility and changed my life forever. Kayla is now a graduate of Ohio State University with a degree in Actuarial Science and works and lives in New York. She is employed by New York Life Insurance as an Actuary Associate. God will work everything out!

The Beginning of Something Life-Changing

I headed off to college with a group of guys who were determined to make it happen and to finish what we started. My Talladega crew included Tyrish (Pete) Garrett, Jeremy Spratling (the black Brad Pitt), Terrence Hall, Anthony Lewis, and Terrance Turner. We were not going to be dropouts and go back home—though you might not have known this during our first week on campus—but we hung out together and learned what it took to survive away from home for the first time.

One of my professors made a profound statement that I carry with me to this day: "In every situation, the cream always rises to the top." For me, this means that you might not be the best in the beginning, but if you do the work, put the time in, and do what's right, you will come to the top every time. This statement has become part of my personal philosophy.

One day, I met up with my group of Talladega friends. They were hanging out with some guys I didn't know, but I soon discovered there was something about them I liked. They were go-getters just like I am. That day, I met Ramone Harper, Marc Desgraves, Bryant Spencer, and Herman Moncrief. As we got to know one another, it seems we were always getting together for one reason or another, and we always had meat on the grill and drinks in the fridge.

This group of friends would become known as TallaDallas. Some of us were as unpolished and rough around the edges as could be; but we were savvy enough to operate, even with limited exposure, and make it in a new world. Ramone, who was from Dallas, Texas, by way of Detroit, Michigan, led this new group. He hosted cookouts that went from just a few people to huge gatherings with hot girls, an incentive for any guy to drop by. With a newfound entrepreneurial spirit, we started to charge admission for the parties; and our company, TDI, was born.

Several years into my college career, I came into my own. As the father of a toddler, my student life was extremely busy. I worked a number of jobs while being in school full-time, so I had to be selective about the events I participated in because of my tight schedule. I maintained a 3.2 GPA, and my focus was razor-sharp; but my personal life was in disarray and filled with many distractions.

Academically, I found my schoolwork to be fairly easy to master, but personally I just couldn't seem to settle down and focus. During that time, I was not such a good father, although I was taking care of my financial responsibilities; but it would take more time for me to become a better dad.

On April 15, 1996, I had an eye-opening experience I'll never forget. My friends and I had spent a fun weekend in Daytona, Florida; but as I was driving back home, I saw my life of good and bad flash before me.

> It was one of the first times I felt moved by God to do anything, so I obeyed His voice.

It was then that I knew it was time for me to do something different. The single life was too much for me. I realized just how much I wanted to graduate, settle down, and become what God had destined for me to be. When I got home, I couldn't stop thinking about my strange vision.

Later, I was notified that I was invited to participate in the Honors Day program. I was being honored for my academic achievements. I thought about not going, but something told me to go. It was one of the first times I felt moved by God to do anything, so I obeyed His voice. Here I was being honored for academics, even though I didn't choose an advanced degree in high school. God can change things around when you have faith, and faith is how I made it.

After the program, I was standing outside with my friend Pete when a beautiful woman came up to me. She said, "You are very handsome," and then she walked away. I stood for a moment, frozen in awe, before running off to find her. After I teased her for complimenting me and then walking away, she told me her name and that she worked at a department store. If I wanted to know any more about her, I would have to meet her at work.

That day, I attended an honors ceremony that I didn't want to attend, but God told me to do it anyway. By being obedient to Him, I met the love of my life, Lykesia Valencia Pringle. Our first date was at the William Shakespeare Theatre in Montgomery, Alabama, where we walked and talked late into the evening. Later that month, I was at Pilgrim Rest Missionary Baptist Church in Montgomery, when I looked down from the balcony and saw a ray of light on her and her mother. At that moment, I knew she was going to be my wife. It was one of the greatest moments of my life.

Ever since my return from Daytona, I was ready to settle down and follow God's plan for my life. My TallaDallas friends and I were expanding the business aspect of our friendship, and we were hosting bigger parties and making more money. However, we were nearing graduation, so we were putting our relationships to the side in order to focus on our careers. Even then, we still gathered as much as we could.

Many of our gatherings were centered on our life changes. First, there were our weddings, so there were the bachelor parties beforehand. When we got together, it was just like we had been together every day. We had so much common ground and so many passions that we shared that our bond was undeniable. We knew we were destined to be business partners as well as friends for life. Even after we left school, we still held one another accountable just like we had done before.

Back to the Present

As my memories fade from my mind, I find myself back at Liberty Hill Missionary Baptist Church, preparing to take the pulpit and address the lively congregation. The memories of how I got here make me more excited because I know that many times, things looked bad in my life. But the Bible reminds me that though weeping may endure for a night, joy comes in the morning. The Word of God also tells me to count it all joy when one falls into divers temptations.

> We had so much common ground and so many passions that we shared that our bond was undeniable.

I count it joy when I think about how I have been able to complete a master's degree and a doctorate in educational leadership, policy, and law. I have been to Capitol Hill to lobby before Congress. I have counseled, advised, and mentored thousands of students all over the Southeast; and I have ministered throughout Georgia and Alabama. I have consulted with businesses, colleges, and nonprofits around the country and written grants totaling well over $10 million—all of this from a man who was raised in Talladega, Alabama. More importantly, I am the father of four amazing children, Kayla Donielle, Brencleveton Donta II, Tyler Ashley, and Amber Lydia. I have been blessed, but it was not easy.

I now move to the pulpit and read Judges 6:15: "And he said unto him, Oh my Lord, wherewith shall I save Israel? behold, my family is poor in Manasseh, and I am the least in my father's house. And the LORD said unto him, Surely I will be with thee." Like Gideon, I can say, "God has been with me!"

CHAPTER TWO

BORN SINNER, OPPOSITE OF A WINNER
RAMONE HARPER

Heavy breathing. Yelling. Loud cry. That was a familiar scene during the night when my father would wake up from what seemed like a nightmare. Later, he told me he was dreaming that he saw his father in heaven, and he was sitting in a chair with an empty chair next to him. My father would cry because his father seemed so lonely up there by himself, and there was nothing he could do about it.

For years, my father was troubled by what others used to tell him when he was younger. They said he would be a preacher just like his father. He hated it and ran from it because he knew it wasn't for him.

This is the dream that haunted Raymond Maye his whole life. Raymond was born on May 20, 1945, to Minister James Earl Maye and Annie Maye. He was the youngest boy of nine siblings. James Earl would get up early in the morning and come in late at night, constantly on the go due to his work and ministry life. He was told to slow down, but he didn't listen, and he ended up having triple bypass heart surgery. One night, James Earl was in bed, and he came up out of the bed about three feet. When he came back down, that was it; his heart just gave out.

Raymond married at an early age but quickly divorced. He also had a daughter from a brief relationship. Since he didn't have a relationship with the mother, unfortunately, he didn't have a good relationship with his daughter, either.

Barbara Jean Harper was separated from her husband and had two children when she met Raymond. The relationship was doomed from the start because they clearly had two different views of what it meant to be in a relationship. Although Raymond spent a lot of time with Barbara and her children, he wasn't taking care of his own daughter.

Into this tumultuous relationship, I was born on December 13, 1975. My parents weren't married, and now they had a new baby boy—Ramone Earl Harper. Raymond loved being a father, but he didn't want legal responsibility, so he didn't sign my birth certificate. Instead, my mother's husband's name was put there, so I ended up a Harper instead of a Maye. Needless to say, I was born at the height of our family drama.

Despite being born in sin in a neighborhood where most African American men were not considered to amount to anything, God had His hand on me. Under those circumstances, my options were grim: dead by 21, a dope dealer or user, a thug, a high school dropout, in prison, or worse. Though my percentages were not good, I still had hope.

When I looked at my bloodline, I saw that my paternal grandfather was a minister, my paternal grandmother was a deaconess, and my maternal great-grandfather was a minister. Then there was my maternal grandmother who was an illegal entrepreneur who ran numbers and sold Avon.

Let me explain.

I never knew what my grandmother did, but she always had a lot of money all over the house; and some of the most unique people would visit her while I was there on the weekends— from men in business suits to funny-looking men with colored suits and hats to women of every kind. I never had the nerve to ask what she did, but all I know is she had respect, and the neighborhood kids were banned from playing with me. My mother had an entrepreneurial spirit, and my father was an entrepreneur. So what would be my destiny? A combination of them all!

The Motown Influence

I grew up in Detroit in between Wayne State University and Motown Studios, which is where I developed my love for music. I thought my dad was a celebrity or someone important because we always went to the best restaurants, he dressed well, and it seems everyone knew him. At the time, I didn't understand why he was surrounded by so many beautiful women; but they loved him, and they loved me. His special relationship with the opposite sex intrigued me, and I didn't realize until later how much of a stronghold this was for the men in my family. This had a major impact on me. Let's just say, the apple doesn't fall too far from the tree.

When my dad moved from Detroit to Colorado, I was upset with him. It didn't help that he and my mom were going through rough times.

My mom would not allow me to see him because she was angry with him, but he would try to come to the house anyway. From kindergarten until the third grade, I don't remember seeing him very often or talking to him that much. His absence caused me to form a coping mechanism that wouldn't allow me to value relationships or get too close to anyone or anything because of my fear of losing them.

When my oldest brother went to the Army and my sister went away to private school, I decided that I wouldn't let anyone get close to me because I thought they would eventually leave me or not be there to support me. So I would give people the cold shoulder and cut them off quickly before they could abandon me.

My mom dated a man who was a big-time radio disc jockey in Detroit. He was a local celebrity of sorts, and it seemed as if everyone knew him. He treated my mother well, and we benefited from that; but he wasn't much of a father figure. In fact, I can't remember any conversations we ever had when I was a child, but I did appreciate him getting us tickets to all the best concerts (Patti Labelle, Luther Vandross, Shalamar, and Prince, just to name a few).

Although my mother's boyfriend and I didn't talk much, he did something even better, he exposed me to music and entertainment, which allowed me to see how celebrities lived. By allowing me to go backstage and meet different artists, I saw something different than all the crime and poverty in my neighborhood, and I decided that I wanted that lifestyle for myself. Those experiences influenced me then and continue to inspire me today. I believe that in order for young people to *be* something different, they must *see* something different and be exposed to better options.

Things in my life changed, though, after local neighborhood gang members with loaded guns chased me because I was involved in beating up one of their members at the swimming pool. That was the scariest thing I have ever experienced. I thought for sure my life was over, and I wasn't even in the fifth grade! When my mom found out, coupled with the fact that my older brother and sister were no longer home to protect me, she called my dad and told him that he had his wish: I could live with him.

> Although it took having my life threatened to end up with my father, this was the best thing that could have ever happened to me.

Although it took having my life threatened to end up with my father, this was the best thing that could have ever happened to me. Before I knew it, I was on a plane to Dallas. My dad's words had actually come true, and he had kept his promise that one day I would live with him. I had finally found my hero—not Superman, not He-Man, but my dad.

From that time on, he told me to tell him the truth and never lie to him. He assured me that if I was always honest with him, he would always defend me and have my back. He was my true mentor, and he taught me many of the life lessons I live by today. Because of my father, I never wanted a tattoo, never had a pierced ear, stopped wearing sagging pants, treated young women with respect, worked hard at being a gentleman, focused on my education so that I could have options in my adult life, and so much more.

My father was not without his faults, though. He struggled with having successful relationships and controlling his temper. However, he had so many other great qualities. He was willing to teach me principles so I could make up my own mind about life, and that has been invaluable to me. He took me to the finest hotels and restaurants to expose me to another way of life and showed me that I could do and have anything.

He challenged me to be great and to be careful about the company I kept. He took time to teach and pour into my friends, so much so that he became a mentor to them and provided them with some of their first jobs. I realized that having a father made a difference. My other friends loved to come over to our house and soak up the wisdom he would give them. As a teenager, I didn't think his advice was that great; but to my friends who didn't have positive male role models, his wisdom and advice were like priceless gems.

However, as a man, I now spend my life giving back to others through ministry and mentoring because I know this makes the difference in developing strong men and leaders today. The old adage is true: "It takes a man to raise a man."

In high school, I was co-captain of the basketball team, and I developed life-long friendships. Just like I did in middle school, I built a crew of like-minded friends that served as my surrogate family. Because my biological family was often in disarray, I decided that I would pick my own family. I treated my friends like brothers and loved them with everything I had.

Once I reached high school, my friends and I developed a new crew called the Teddy Bear Crew. We were bonded by our love for sports and women. The name of our group came from the sexual escapades of one of the guys. He told us that you know you have a girl when you can make her make out with a teddy bear in front of you. This revelation blew our minds! So we challenged ourselves to see how far we could take our game and then have extreme stories to report back to the crew.

I know, I know—such a sick mindset for a young teenager to have, but that was the way it was for me. That bend in my bloodline toward womanizing was resurfacing, and it was especially strong in my teenage years. It was so strong that it became a chink in my male armor, and it began to define me.

Relationships Are Everything

Despite my thinking as a teenager, I developed a keen sense of the value of relationships that has always been a key to my success. As an adult, I now understand that when you want to get something done, it isn't always what you know but who you know. When we conduct our DREAMS seminars, we focus on relationships as a key aspect because those who understand the importance of relationships and are able to leverage them are able to achieve their goals without taking advantage of people.

In the eleventh grade, I fell in love for the first time. I remember it like it was yesterday. One day, my friends and I went back to my old middle school to play basketball. There I saw this unique and pretty girl. Although she was with a group of girls, she stood out like a rock star. She was the leader of the pack like I was in my crew; and even though she was younger than I was, she had unbelievable confidence.

By my senior year, she and I were head-over-heels in love. We were the best of friends and spent all of our time together. She even started hanging out with my friends. It was this early relationship that taught me what it meant to love another person, sacrifice for someone, and treat a woman with the utmost respect. She would have it no other way. However, I had to begin my transition to college, which meant we would be apart for the first time. It was because of her that I knew I wanted to go college and make something of my life so I could make her proud, but little did I know that this girl would change my life for good and bad.

My aunt was the college coordinator at our church, Mt. Olive. She would coordinate college tours and help students with financial aid and scholarship searches. I went on my first historical black college tour during my senior year, and it was the start of my dream.

Mr. Duncan, my tour guide, believed that the best way to prepare students for life was to expose them to people, places, and things outside of their regular environment. This principle would arise time and time again in my life and become part of my own worldview.

On the college tour of historically black colleges and universities (HBCUs), we visited Morehouse College and

Clark Atlanta in Georgia, and Norfolk State and Hampton University in Virginia. By the time I got back home, my mind was made up: I was going to Hampton University. I had never seen such a beautiful site: African American men and beautiful women studying, hanging out, partying—all in a safe environment near the beach. Did I mention beautiful women? I should have said *fine* women! During the last semester of my senior year, I received notice that I was accepted to Hampton.

The bad news was that I would have to take out a loan or pay for some of the expenses myself. I was still determined to go, and my dad was preparing to support me. Despite my insistence on going to Hampton, my aunt told me to apply to plenty of other schools, which was the wisest thing I could have done. I had no idea at the time what she was doing, but she and Mr. Duncan were showing me what mentorship looks like.

After I graduated with honors from Bowie High in 1993, I spent my summer preparing for college. Aunt Gloria called to tell me that she could help me get a full academic scholarship to Alabama State University, a school I knew nothing about. So guess what I did?

The Golden Years

Experts say the height of hip-hop music spanned from about the mid-1980's to the mid-1990's. This "golden age" was characterized by its diversity, quality, innovation, and influence. The music's subject matter varied while the music itself was experimental and included eclectic sampling. Gangsta rap hit the scene with groups such as Geto Boys, N.W.A., Dr. Dre, and Death Row. One of the uniting factors of my high school friends, the Teddy Bear Crew, and my soon-to-be-developed crew in college was our love for music.

When I graduated high school, *The Chronic* had taken over the mainstream music industry and would introduce us to stars such as Snoop Dogg, Tupac, and The Notorious B.I.G. This music provided the backdrop for my entry into Alabama State University in the fall of 1993. Referring to hip-hop in its golden age, *Spin* magazine's editor-in-chief, Sia Michel, says, "There were so many important, groundbreaking albums coming out right about that time." MTV's Sway Calloway adds, "The thing that made that era so great is that nothing was contrived. Everything was still being discovered and everything was still innovative and new."

As a full-scholarship freshman on the campus of ASU, I realized how different my life was now. I had moved from Dallas-Fort Worth, a large metropolitan city, to Montgomery, Alabama, the home of the Civil Rights Movement. Then, while living in Benson Hall, I thought that this was the worst decision I had ever made.

There were community showers, no phones in the rooms (we had to share a pay phone at the end of the hall), and there were black people all over the place—talk about culture shock! Some rooms had three to five guys living in a small quarter, which was like prison to me. Plus, I was missing the love of my life back home. So I did what any homesick kid would do: I called my dad and told him to come and get me, ASAP!

BORN SINNER, OPPOSITE OF A WINNER

There were a few bright spots that kept me at peace, though. Thanks to Aunt Gloria, a few of my friends from home attended ASU that year, too. There was also a childhood friend of my family at ASU. He was a fellow graduate and athlete from my high school. I knew him back then only because he was a basketball rival I played against in middle school and high school, but he quickly became my best friend.

Then my freshman roommate, Terrence Hall, helped me not be quite so homesick. Terrence was from a small town called Talladega, Alabama; and he was the funniest, smartest, countriest cat I had ever met. He and his friends from Talladega would eventually make up the foundation of a life-long friendship and crew affectionately called TallaDallas.

Trust Issues

Just when I thought my first year away from home would be an overwhelming success, I then experienced my first heartbreak, which almost brought me to my knees.

My high school sweetheart, who was still in high school, became pregnant, and my life was turned upside down. From the beginning, I wanted to be a good father, so I decided I would transfer to another school so I could be closer to her and the baby. After the child was born, however, I found out on Father's Day—of all days—that the baby wasn't mine and that she had had a relationship with someone else while I was away at school. As hurtful as that news was to me, I had to acknowledge that I hadn't exactly been faithful to her, either, and it was my infidelity to our relationship that caused her to seek revenge by being with someone else.

I loved her; but she had abandoned me, and it hurt like hell!

This hurt led to my first real encounter with a God that I hadn't paid much attention to. I was upset, angry, ashamed, and confused; and I reacted the way most immature Christians do. I cried out, "God, how could you do this to me?" During that time, I spent many long nights binge drinking and sleeping with multiple women, thinking I could cure the pain and get back at all the women in my life who had caused me pain. The very thing I feared happened: I had allowed someone to get close to me, and I loved her; but she had abandoned me, and it hurt like hell!

Eventually, I healed from this heartbreak and moved on with someone else. This woman was a close friend from Arlington who had witnessed what I had gone through, so I felt like a relationship with her was a safe move and would be my saving grace. She and I started off strong, and I even attended church more consistently with her. All was well for a few months, but then I found out she had cheated on me with an old boyfriend.

She was sorry about hurting me and wanted to do all she could to make it up to me and earn my forgiveness, but back then I knew nothing about forgiveness. I just felt more pain and heartbreak. This time, however, I resolved that women could never be trusted, so I was just going to live my life how I wanted to with no regards for others or for God.

So Close to the Dream

My only consolation during these difficult times was school and my TallaDallas boys. I excelled in my grades and maintained a 4.0 GPA during my first two years. In 1997, I graduated magna cum laude from ASU with a degree in communications and a concentration in public relations.

TallaDallas started as a group of wet-behind-the-ears freshmen from two totally different worlds, and we became a family of brothers who would bond together to accomplish amazing feats. One of the unique features of TDI was that we showed love for everybody. Unlike the various wars and battles going on in the world, and even on campus, TDI stood for love and brotherhood.

Our brotherhood was forged during the huge hip-hop battle between East Coast and West Coast. The Notorious B.I.G. and Bad Boy Records led the East Coast, and Tupac and Death Row Records led the West. Unfortunately, their feud led to the death of Biggie and 2pac, two of the greatest MCs to ever touch a microphone. Biggie's lyrical legacy will remain forever, as he is affectionately remembered as "the King of New York." His timeless lyrics, which provided the soundtrack for our youth, are the inspiration for this book.

On the college scene, the 1990's were a time when Greek life was disjointed and segregated. Many of the Greek organizations were suspended on the campuses of HBCUs because of dangerous hazing incidents. A student in Florida was killed while pledging. At ASU, there was a split in fraternities and sororities that made no sense. So-called "real Greeks" pledged the traditional way, while "paper Greeks" decided to join the new way, which didn't require the rigorous demands of normal pledging.

Despite the animosity in Greek life at ASU, TDI wasn't anti-Greek. Terrence Hall was the first member of our crew to pledge. He was followed by Jeremy (Omega Psi Phi); Donta, Anthony, and Tyrish (Kappa Alpha Psi); and Terrance Turner (Alpha Phi Alpha). Still, Greek life was surrounded by a lot of negativity and division back then, so TDI became the one organization on campus that people could count on for unity, brotherhood, and love. We spread love to everyone, no matter his or her affiliation or method of pledging (or lack thereof). Even at our parties, we extended special invitations to all Greeks, and we set up VIP tables for the sororities. The fact that fights would break out between the "real" and "paper" soros wasn't our problem!

As a crew, the members of TDI did everything together at ASU. We partied, traveled, and studied together. We also spent spring breaks and other holidays with one another's families. We hosted family dinners at one another's apartments on Sunday nights to make sure we stayed connected, as well as making sure no one had to go without eating if money was tight.

We built a reputation on campus as party guys, but what most people didn't know was that almost everyone of us was excelling with all A's and B's. Terrence Hall, Terrance Turner, and I were part of an honors program that allowed us to travel with the school to different colleges for research and other programs. Together we did everything. I can't begin to write down all of the foolish shenanigans we got into. Some of them were downright criminal.

I started this chapter by talking about being born a sinner. Well, I was born into sin, and then there were some sins that followed me throughout my life, becoming even more apparent during my time at college. They say an idle mind is the devil's playground. For my group of friends, there must have been a lot of boring and idle times. We were extremely lucky because we all could have been arrested, or we could have even been shot. Thankfully, by our sophomore and junior years, we found jobs and legitimate ways of making money by throwing parties off campus.

We started our entrepreneurial journey by organizing some of the best parties in Montgomery. We threw upscale parties at apartment clubhouses, and eventually we became so popular that we had to move to The Governors House Hotel. We capitalized on our influence on campus by promoting our parties in class, at sporting events, on the yard during lunch when the DJ was blasting the music, at nightclubs like Top Flight (The Rose), and other places. We were definitely ahead of our time. We even had VIP tables for all the women from various sororities and hired the best DJ in the city, DJ Ced.

On campus, we were known as The Red Hat Boys because our signature look included red Texas Ranger hats, blue blazers, and khakis. Not only did we charge an entrance fee to our parties, we also had a specific dress code to keep the riffraff out. The parties afforded us the opportunity to travel to events such as Freaknic in Atlanta, strip clubs in Georgia, and the Black College Reunion in Daytona Beach, Florida.

One of our greatest joys was what people remembered about us the most, we knew how to party. Whatever event or party you could think of in the South, TDI was probably there. Black college weekend in Daytona? Multiple times. Freaknic in Atlanta? Done. Statewide step show in Tuscaloosa? Check. Magic City Classic? Yep. Turkey Day Classic? Did it. Bayou Classic in New Orleans? Of course. Kappa Lua at Florida A&M? We were there. Tennessee State University homecoming? Yes. Tuskegee homecoming? We owned it (NBDSGB was life-changing).

However, the business side of TDI on the party scene was birthed out of house parties under the guidance of one of our original TDI members, Mike McKinney, aka Primetime, and his cousin. Our first parties were at their house seemingly every month. Mike was from Talladega and went to ASU before most of us. What started as a hangout spot and BBQ became larger than life. Students would hang out with the TallaDallas boys and pack out the house and the driveway.

One day, while congregating at my honors dorm, McGinty Apartments, the lights went off. We needed to take it up a notch and throw a real party, so we decided to rent out a clubhouse somewhere and do it right.

One Friday night, we had our trial run at Red Lion Apartments. We had printed up fliers and invited everyone we knew on campus, so the scene was thick. We had bartenders, food, a DJ, and smoke. (Well, not official smoke, but you get the idea. It was hazy in the room.) About two hours into the party, someone told our crew to come out to the parking lot to see how many people were waiting to get inside. It looked like Freaknic all over again in the streets of Piedmont Park! If a light went off at McGinty, then a siren was blaring at Red Lion. We saw the light and the possibility that we could do this in real life. So we continued to charge, and the rest is history.

We made a lot of mistakes during our college years and committed all type of sinful acts that I know my parents and professors wouldn't be proud of. Whatever struggles and mistakes that our youth are doing today, we probably saw the movie and bought the t-shirt so nothing surprises me when we speak to them across this country during our D.R.E.A.M.S. Seminar. That is why we are able to come together today to help share our mistakes and pitfalls with other young men so they don't have to do the same things. I want them to know that after everything I did, God still had a plan for me, and He has a plan for them, too.

After graduating from ASU, I accepted a position with the Environmental Protection Agency in Houston, Texas, as part of the New Leader Program. I was the first African American man to be hired under this program in that region. It was at this time that I had an encounter with God that would change my life forever.

Late one night, I was watching Bishop T. D. Jakes on television. It was like he was speaking directly to me and telling me that the only reason I was able to do so much dirt and not suffer the consequences (jail, diseases, or other disappointments) was because someone was praying for me. That night in October 1997, I accepted Christ as my personal Lord and Savior.

Then It Happened

After years of battling cancer, my father gave up. On May 1, 2010, he went home to be with the Lord; and I lost my mentor, my role model, my best friend, and one of my top supporters. The pain I experienced that day was unlike any other. My family was there to support me, and my TallaDallas brothers were at my side the entire time.

It was then that I remembered how my dad's nightmares ended. After years of waking up from the nightmare of seeing his father in heaven, suffering alone with an empty chair next to him and not understanding what it meant, my father told me that when I accepted my call to ministry, the next time he had that dream, he slept in peace. What did he see? In one chair, he saw my grandfather, smiling, and he saw me sitting next to him. At that point, he said he knew everything would be all right.

Though I lost my mentor a few years ago, I know I will see him again, and I will continue his legacy of mentoring by helping as many young men as I can. That is why Turning Dreams Into Realities means so much to me. God surrounded me with men who shared similar passions so that we could help inspire a new generation of successful African American men.

Despite my shaky upbringing, having the odds stacked against me, overcoming my shortcomings and moral failures such as violating God's instructions that warns against premarital sex, I have found a level of success, and my dreams are just beginning. I have started my own management and consulting company; helped develop the careers of some award-winning entertainers; and helped others start successful businesses, ministries, and nonprofit organizations. Currently, I also serve as an executive pastor at my church located in New Jersey.

It all started with a dream, and now our desire is to help turn the dreams of others into reality.

CHAPTER THREE

AGAINST ALL ODDS
BRYANT SPENCER

As I prepare to enter my forties, I take time to reflect on my life. I think about where I started, where I am, how I got here, and where I might go.

Today, I'm an executive at a Fortune 10 company; I'm married to a beautiful, loving wife; and I spilt my time between two cities I call home. I have had the opportunity to travel all across the country and halfway around the world. I've vacationed in some of the most desirable locations.

To some people, this may seem ordinary or lackluster. To others, this may sound boastful. To me, it shows that although you are from meager and humble beginnings, you can defy the odds. To understand this, you must know where I'm from. You must know my story.

Where I Started

As the summer of 1975 came to a close, I was born in Aliceville, Alabama, to a single mother. Aliceville is a small town in Pickens County, along the border with Mississippi. I grew up in an even smaller town known as Pickensville. It was such a small town that it didn't have its own zip code. The county has less than 20,000 residents, and the income per capita is less than $14,000 annually.*

In Pickensville, the statistics are worse. There are about 600 residents, and 34 percent of them live below the poverty line.* My family was no exception. As you can imagine, the odds weren't in my favor from the start.

Although I was faced with an uphill battle just by the sheer nature of the hand I was dealt, I did have a few things in my favor, mainly my family. My mother and grandparents worked hard early on to teach me the basic fundamentals of life such as the difference between right and wrong and having faith in the Lord. We were poor, but I never went without the essentials. I missed out on many of my wants, but my family always took care of my needs. I never went without food, shelter, or clothing on my back. This may not sound like much to some people, but it meant the world to me as I watched others struggle with such challenges.

Knowing that my family was going to make sure our needs were met inspired me. This strengthened the bond with my mother and grandparents, but this bond also caused me to be shy and somewhat of an introvert. As a child, I never felt comfortable being away from my family. They were my security blanket, and I didn't want to be too far away from them.

Another extension of my family were my godparents, who served as an influence on my learning and growth. Although they were older than my grandparents, they treated me like their own son, perhaps because they didn't have any children of their own. I spent a large part of my summers with them. They owned a farm that was filled with livestock and crops. Although the summer heat was brutal, I enjoyed working on the farm equipment, fishing in the creek, and learning to live on the fruits of one's labor.

Although my godparents' economic situation was like that of most people in that area, they didn't allow it to be a crutch. Their humbleness and slow-paced lifestyle worked well with my personality. I used this time to learn how to drive, change a tire, and to perform other basic automotive skills—all of which were pretty exciting for a young person like me.

Other than my mother, grandparents, and godparents, good role models were hard to come by. There weren't many people to look up to or aspire to emulate. With jobs being so scarce in such a low-income community, being an educator or joining the military seemed to be the best career—if you didn't count small-town drug dealing. Like most of America during the 1980's, my small town wasn't immune to crack and other drugs that were prevalent in more urban areas.

Since being a teacher, joining the military, or being a drug dealer were last on my career list, I knew I had to have a better plan if I was going to stay in the area. If I didn't, I would have to leave home to make something of myself. After graduating high school in Pickens County, the biggest achievement was to own your own trailer that you could park behind your parent's house. However, most people ended up putting mobile homes behind mobile homes, creating pseudo trailer parks. Parked in front of the ideal trailer was a S-10 Chevy low-rider with a booming system.

The dream job was working in the tire factory or the lumber factory for over ten dollars an hour, plus overtime and an annual raise of ten cents an hour. If you had all of this, life was good. If you're from somewhere else this simple living might seem like an easily obtainable goal, but in our community it was rare. Such a living was cherished by those who obtained it and envied by those who didn't.

Marriage wasn't a goal, but having children seemed to be a race to see who could have the most at the youngest age. Teen pregnancy was common—so common that it seemed welcomed, and maybe even encouraged. Well-known psychiatrist Phil McGraw, better known as Dr. Phil, wrote an article called "The Real Teen Mom: Alarming Statistics." He says, "Daughters of teen moms are three times more likely to become teenage mothers themselves." This is what makes it so difficult to end the cycle or get out of the trap.

In the same article, Dr. Phil also cites, "The sons of teen moms are two times more likely to end up in prison. Children who live apart from their fathers are also five times more likely to be poverty-stricken than children with both parents at home." Since I was born to a teen mother, and I lived apart from my father, I can say with confidence that I rose above the statistics and against the odds. I haven't been to prison, and I haven't been impoverished.

Now that you have a sense of where I started, now you need to understand my foundation and the experiences that shaped me. In order to give myself more options and increase my chances of having a better life than that of those around me, I knew that I had to be better than my peers. Early on, I was performing above average in school, and I didn't have to over extend myself in order to have success in the classroom. Unfortunately, I didn't have anyone to help me excel or to push me. I tended to settle for A's and mostly B's instead of striving to do my best all the time.

Even at this level, I was doing better than most; but I realized that I would be more successful if I surrounded myself with like-minded people. Since I wanted to be and considered myself to be above average, I wanted to be around others who had the same ambitions so I could escape the trap that I called home. My hometown was a trap because of the lack of ambition that surrounded me.

My first opportunity to meet other ambitious and successful people came through my new church. At a young age, I was allowed to go to a church that my mother and grandparents didn't attend. Although the church was still in the general area, the members' mindset and worldview were different from what I knew to be the norm.

The majority of the members were what I would consider pillars of the community. They came from a number of professional fields: medical, education, business, and the military, just to name a few. I was deeply inspired by this congregation because they opened my eyes not only to other occupations, but I was able to see people who looked like me thrive in those positions.

At the same time I was broadening my social awareness, I was able to form and build a relationship with Christ. Some people might shrug off my faith as something relatively minor, but for me it was a big deal and was something I desperately needed.

Although I was from a background and lineage completely different from theirs, the members of my church community welcomed me with open arms. Initially, I felt out of place. The church service was different from what I was accustomed to. Their music was different, the lights were brighter, the facility wasn't rundown, and there weren't multiple collection plates and offering requests. Church didn't last from sunup to sundown.

> I told her that I didn't know and that she should ask someone without insurance.

I don't know what interest the family that introduced me to the church had in me. Sometimes I think they looked at me as a project of some sort, and to some degree, I'm sure that I was. This was their way of helping and giving back to someone who may have been less fortunate.

My church was a welcoming environment, but it didn't come without doubters, people who didn't think I could rise above the odds. I was shocked when one of my Sunday school teachers tried to use my background as an example in one of her classes.

The lesson was related to doing what's right versus doing what's wrong and being responsible. During the lesson, she started talking about people being irresponsible by driving without insurance and how it puts a financial burden on the rest of us if an accident should occur. Then she asked me how it felt to drive without insurance. I told her that I didn't know and that she should ask someone without insurance.

Not that this was a defining moment in my life, but it was another example of how people viewed me. They thought my circumstances defined me and that I should be put in a box along with everyone else who came from a similar background.

Because I was surrounded by such successful people at church, I was inspired to go into the world of business. During my junior year in high school, I researched the types of careers in business to see what I wanted to do. I asked one of my teachers what were some of the highest paying careers. The answer was CEO. This reinforced my desire to start a career in business.

In order to be successful in business, I knew college was going to be a requirement, but I still toyed with the idea of going to work first and then pursuing my education. While I was contemplating this, my mother gave me the motivation and advice I needed. She told me that I had to go to work or go to school, but I couldn't stay at home for free.

When I told her my plan to go to work first and then go to school, she told me that if I started working that I would never go to school because once money started coming in and I started spending it, I would never give it up to get an education. As always, my mother was right. So I looked at my options for college.

I was tops in my class, but I still ran into doubters—this time they were my teachers. They tried to encourage me to go to junior college or maybe a trade school so that I would have a better chance for success; but I guess one of my teachers did have a little faith in me. She said, "When I first met you,

I didn't think that you would amount to a hill of beans. But now I believe that you can attend a four-year university." I wasn't sure what to make of her comment, so I looked at her awkwardly, thanked her, and walked away. I had a plan in place, and now it was time to execute the first phase.

As I prepared for college, I focused on my GPA, community service, and extracurricular activities. I knew that I was in no position to pay for college, so if I was going to attend, I had to get there by pursuing scholarships.

During my senior year, I spent many days and nights looking for scholarships. I worked with the school's guidance counselor to identify potential opportunities. He wasn't much help. I guess he didn't get those types of questions that often. I couldn't rely on my parents and grandparents to assist me with my journey. I was the first to go to college and had to figure it out on my own, which included figuring out what school to attend, how to apply, how to pay for it, and all the other steps in between.

I attended a few college fairs, which were helpful. I took a rudimentary approach to narrowing down colleges. First, I considered my financial situation, so I knew that I had to look for economical options. Second, I compared the distance from home. The school had to be within driving distance, but I didn't want to be too close to home.

Third, I had to find out how much room and board would cost. Fourth, I had to look at out-of-state fees, which narrowed my search to in-state schools.

Fifth, I discovered that private schools limited my financial aid options, so they were out. I knew that I was going to need every bit of free money I could find. I mostly applied to schools that didn't have an application fee. For the few schools I applied to that required an application fee, I chose them based on the fee amount.

Perhaps some might say this was shortsighted on my part, but I had done my homework. Through my research of different universities, a review of graduation rates, the accreditation of the schools and their academic programs, the average class size, and the earning potential after graduation, I noticed that there was only a small degree of variance between the schools that I was looking to attend.

I applied to four schools, and I was accepted to all of them. Now it was decision time. From the start, I was leaning toward attending a historically black college and university (HBCU); but as a kid, I dreamed of going to the University of Alabama, which was essentially in my backyard. As I got older and learned more about the school, I wasn't as interested. Out of my four options, Alabama State University met all of my criteria.

Where I Went

During my sophomore year at ASU, I was able to surround myself with a new group of like-minded people. These were newfound brothers for me. We encouraged one another and looked out for one another. They helped me focus, and our bond actually helped me to become a better student.

I started to focus on what I was going to do after college, and I put myself in the best position for success after college. I found a job on campus in the career development center, which was ideal because it gave me the chance to use work time to improve my resume writing and to learn interview techniques. I was able to see which companies were coming to recruit on campus before most of the other students, which gave me an advantage. I was able to secure a paid internship the summer before my junior year.

Then just a few weeks into my senior year, I had another odd but defining moment. I was able to secure a job that I would start after graduation. The reason this is significant is because I didn't have to worry about what I was going to do after graduation. I didn't have the same worries as most of my friends and the other seniors who were graduating. It was a good feeling going through my entire senior year without this worry or fear. It gave me time to look at other potential options, such as other employment opportunities and graduate school. Now all I had to do was graduate, but this proved to be more challenging than I had imagined.

Three weeks before graduation, I found out that I wasn't going to receive a final grade in one of my marketing classes. Obviously, without a final grade I wouldn't be eligible for graduation. This was a big disappointment. After all of my hard work, and after all of that time, and after overcoming so many obstacles and defying the odds, I was about to fall short, become another statistic, and—most of all—disappoint my family. I knew that my journey was also their journey. This was just as much their graduation as it was mine, and I was about to let us all down.

What about the career I had waiting for me? Was it lost as well? Would I have to start over? Was I about to share the same concerns and fears as many other seniors—what to do after graduation?

As the days passed, I became more discouraged and more restless. I finally called my mother and gave her the news. Just as I expected, she was disappointed and felt like I had robbed her of a college graduation, something that she had been looking forward to since the day I was born. After hearing my mother's pain, I had to do something. I couldn't just sit idly by and let this take place. I decided to take matters into my own hands.

I talked to the professor, who was also the dean. He justified why he didn't give me a grade. He explained that my disregard for the educational process caused him to delay my graduation. It didn't look like I was going to convince him otherwise until I asked for advice. I asked him what I should tell my future employer. He said incredulously, "Your employer? You have a job?" Once I told him I did, his tone seemed to change, but his message didn't. I left not knowing what to expect.

The following week, I learned that I had received my grade, and I was eligible for graduation. After hearing the news, I couldn't wait to tell my family, especially my mother. I wish I could have seen the relief on her face. Now all was restored and back on track.

However, my life after college seemed to be just as much of a challenge as the other transitions in my life. After graduation, I immediately began my professional career. I found a job with a company that moved me from Pickensville, Alabama, to Orlando, Florida. As you can imagine, this was a major move for someone from such a small town. Not only had I never been to Orlando, I don't think anyone from my county had been there, either.

To me, Orlando was the largest place on earth. The city was eye-opening, with endless options and countless possibilities. In the beginning, the adjustment was a bit difficult. I was no longer surrounded by college students, and I didn't have the comfort of a college campus to shield me from the world. I was in the real world now.

> # My peers were adults with real-world issues.

My peers were adults with real-world issues. They had families and mortgages, and they were trying to figure out how to send their children to college. This meant that there was no more hanging out after class, no more twelve-hour weeks of class, no more college buddies—just me and a full-time job that I was trying to turn into a career. This is where I found out how much I didn't know, but the things I didn't know were common knowledge to other people.

One instance of my ignorance came at an informal meeting with a few of my co-workers. We were discussing exotic dishes and dining experiences. When it was my turn to talk about an exotic dish, I mentioned a meal I had only a few months before. I told the group I had eaten mahi-mahi. After the laughter stopped, they explained to me that mahi-mahi wasn't exotic. In fact, it was quite common. Let's just say that in Pickensville, no one heard of mahi-mahi, so, yes, it was pretty exotic to me.

However, the lesson I learned that day was that I was in a different place with different people. They weren't like me. They didn't experience the things that I had experienced. Although we were peers, I was still a minority. I had to step up and learn about their world. For the next few years, this became my new focus. Many people refer to this as "playing the game," and I had to learn quickly. If I was going to be in this new world, I would have to learn how to live and work in it.

I spent two and a half years in Orlando and had decent success. I achieved enough success to be promoted to the corporate office just outside of Chicago. If I thought that Orlando was the largest place on earth, Chicago had to be the largest place in the galaxy.

I was able to adjust to my environment quicker in Chicago than I did in Orlando because I made natural, progressive steps. I went from a tiny town in Alabama to a large town in Alabama to a large city in the Southeast to a major city in America. While in Chicago my career flourished. I was in a new role every 18 months or less. I was able to do this because I learned not only how to play the game but how the game was played. I recognized my weaknesses and used the game to offset them.

Unfortunately, for my peers who came from similar backgrounds as mine, they didn't survive. The corporate world is a tough and unforgiving one. You have to be clever to have longevity. You have to be even cleverer if you have a background like mine, and you will need friends along the way.

Recently, I decided to end my professional career in Chicago, and I chose a new career path in New England. This was a tough choice given the fact that I spent most of my professional career in Chicago. I married my wife while in Chicago, and we considered it home. My time in the corporate world has shown me a lot, though. I have traveled all across the country. I have had great social experiences. I have traveled internationally because of my career. I have done a number of things that I don't think I would have done on my own.

My world has expanded vastly since growing up in Pickens County, Alabama. Given where I'm from, I owe a lot to a lot of people; but I owe a lot to myself to keep the drive and determination to strive for more, to never settle, and to dismiss terms or words like *contentment*.

What's Next?

Now that you know where I am, where I'm from, and how I got here, I guess you want to know what's next. The answer to that is, I don't know what's next. What I do know is that it's not over.

I'm still striving toward my original goal from high school of being CEO of a company, or maybe I will find a new goal or a new passion to strive toward. The rest is TBD. Hopefully, through this story you are able to see why my chapter is titled "Against All Odds."

---

*Data based on 2010 census information

CHAPTER FOUR

REACH FOR THE STARS
MARC P. DESGRAVES, CPA

Deoxyribonucleic acid, commonly known as DNA, is the hereditary material in humans and almost all other organisms. Science has shown that humans share 99 percent of the same DNA. Thus, only one percent of each person's DNA is unique. It's amazing to think that such a small percentage of each person's blueprint can have such a significant impact on life experiences, good and bad.

Science has also shown that an important property of DNA is that it can replicate or make copies of itself. It is because of this replication that I believe many people are born with family DNA that creates immediate disadvantages that may not become known until later in life.

My teenage years were spent without much guidance to help in planning for my life or to encourage the evaluation of all options before making decisions. Today I often say, "I didn't know what I didn't know!" As an adult, I've come to discover that part of my family's DNA may be the reason I spent my childhood and college years unguided. I believe that a lack of guidance from a positive male figure shaped my future before I could process and react to reality.

This is a story of needing to dream big, and not allowing adversities to hold you down.

In the Beginning

In March 1975, my father's birthday, I was born into a small family in Davenport, Iowa. My father, Marc Desgraves III (also known as Butch), and my mother, Juanita, were out partying with friends, celebrating my father's birthday, only hours before I was born (which is probably why I love Motown and 1970's music so much). Of course, I don't remember anything from those early days, but many of my parents' friends have said on many occasions that I was a happy baby and was always smiling.

My parents moved to Dallas, Texas, when I was two years old. Before and during my elementary school years, I spent a lot of time in "Sunny South Dallas, where the sun always shines" with my father's aunt, Kathryn Clemons, who everyone affectionately called Ms. Clemons, or Aunt Kitty.

Aunt Kitty helped raise me for long stretches at a time because of my parents' demanding careers. Aunt Kitty was loving and stern at the same time. I was one of those kids who sat at the table for hours until I ate my vegetables, had to pick my own switches from the tree when I needed discipline, and was told several times to stop coming in and out of the house so much because I was "making the bill go up."

Being retired, Aunt Kitty watched a lot of television, which probably explains why I like *The Price Is Right*, *M*A*S*H*, *Gilligan's Island*, *Alice*, and *The Dukes of Hazzard*, among others. Aunt Kitty loved her some Bo and Luke Duke, and I loved me some Daisy! Bob Barker's Beauties weren't too bad to look at either.

The love Aunt Kitty showed was shared by my father's cousin, Uncle Nay, and his entire family. It wasn't until later in life that I discovered that my time with Aunt Kitty, Uncle Nay, and other family members in South Dallas was actually a replication of my father's childhood. Aunt Kitty was married to my father's uncle, Leon Clemons, and they raised my father and his younger brother from the time they were in elementary school until they were in high school in the same house where I spent a lot of my younger years.

My grandfather, Marc Desgraves II, had a career in the Marines, served in World War II, and later worked for the federal government, as did my grandmother, who worked for the Department of Defense for many years doing highly classified work. My father's parents felt it was in their best interest that their children live with Aunt Kitty in Dallas while they focused on their demanding careers on the East Coast.

Ultimately, my father's parents divorced when he was just 11 years old. Similarly, my parents divorced when I was nine and my younger brother was only three. My grandparents' divorce and my parents' divorce shared several common themes, but one of the primary things was that in both cases, there was not a father actively involved in the raising and guiding of the children.

My grandfather's involvement in my father's life may have significantly influenced my father's choice to be absent from my childhood. My father's minimal involvement in my upbringing was not ever anything I resented or complained about because I was always a self-starter and believed I could figure out anything. However, thinking I knew everything and thinking I could tackle any obstacle without any help or guidance was actually one of my main shortcomings.

To her credit, my mother—like many mothers in the past, present, and future—did a good job raising my brother and me. Being a single mother is never easy, and she worked hard at the office and at home. Despite little monetary support from my father, my brother and I didn't go without anything we needed.

Juanita loved unconditionally, taught us right from wrong, attended all our sporting events, and made sure we knew what it meant to be a gentleman. Equally important, my mother taught us certain life skills at a young age, such as how to wash our clothes and cook for ourselves (although I often took the easy way out and fried up some of those cooked bologna sandwiches where the ends curl up).

As wonderful as my mother is, I believe now that without a certain level of confidence and experience, there are just some things that are harder for women to do when raising boys alone. My mother taught us but didn't talk with us often, and most young men and boys need frequent reiteration and verification of understanding.

I received little guidance about setting goals and pursuing my dreams. I didn't have a lot of motivation to excel, and I wasn't challenged and made to think of how to handle many of the situations I would face in life. I didn't have anyone to introduce me to new things or talk about the importance and responsibilities of sex and marriage. I believe it's crucial for an older man with life experience and love in his heart to provide this type of guidance for young men.

One might say that in this country divorce rates are extremely high and children grow up without their fathers all the time, so people should just get over it and move on with life. Looking back on my situation, I would say it wasn't that difficult, and I did a lot of moving on; but I would argue that the long-term effects of the bad choices fathers make have a high likelihood of negative consequences in their children's lives for many years to come.

The Teen Years

If I wasn't in South Dallas with Aunt Kitty, I was at my childhood home in the Oak Cliff neighborhood of Dallas. Both neighborhoods were similar because like most cities with large black populations, it wasn't uncommon to see dogfights, dice games, and street scuffles.

For fear of a good "butt whooping" with a heavy belt buckle or an extension cord, I tried to stay clear of these activities. Besides, there were always cooler things to do, like playing pick-up basketball or football in the street or the forgotten American pastime of wall ball. One of my older friends from the 'hood allowed me to help him throw newspapers from his handlebars, which provided money to make the occasional trip to see the neighborhood candy lady.

Unfortunately, my parents' divorce changed a lot of what went on in our household, and it was difficult for all involved.

Many single parents find themselves in survival mode after a divorce, and it wasn't any different for my mother.

Part of Juanita's survival mode meant packing up our home in Oak Cliff and living in four different cities in three years during the start of my middle school years. One of those stops included living with her sister and her three children in Lancaster, Texas. My mother's sister was also divorced, and I didn't mind staying with my cousins since we saw one another all the time anyway.

Trouble seemed to find us a lot when we were together, though. Whether it was inadvertently destroying something our mothers had just bought us, crashing three-wheelers, or breaking windows with a sling shot, we always had fun and stayed road dogs for one another. That was also the time when hip-hop music was taking off, hairstyles were creative to say the least, and breakdancing was a must—especially on Sunday nights in the middle of the skating rink.

However, that time wasn't all fun and games. In the midst of our moves from one place to another, my mother began dating again. I don't believe anyone in our family liked the man, but my brother and I put up with him while he lived with us.

The intimidation of new schools and changing friends every year wasn't easy, and it was difficult for me to handle the anxiety. I'm almost certain I experienced some level of depression as well for fear of the unknown. It was at this time when I started noticing girls more and could have gotten into some serious trouble if a girl at Lancaster Middle School told anyone about some inappropriate touching I did one day in the school restroom.

I was young and dumb, and this was my first experience with a girl. Given that I hadn't talked with anyone about girls or sex, I didn't know much, and it can be uncomfortable for a young boy to discuss girls and sex with his mother. Those three years of transition and self-discovery would have likely gone a lot better with a positive and responsible male influence in my life.

The last stop during this three-year period was to a brand-new house in Grand Prairie, Texas. My mother used her hard-earned money to buy the house, and the guy she was dating broke it in by growing marijuana in the backyard.

Although the excitement of moving into a new house was high for my brother and me, the adjustment to a new neighborhood, a new school, and new friends was still hard. The only consolation was that in this new house I had my own room again. The transition was also somewhat easier when I met some good friends for life in the neighborhood and joined the basketball team in high school.

Love and Basketball

Basketball became my life; and I would play before school started, for the school team, at home, and on the weekends in any recreation center I could find. Despite not having the guidance of a father who could take me to the park or the court to show me how to play the game, make me work hard, practice my free throws, or encourage me not to be intimidated by anyone, I learned those things by watching others.

I had friends whose fathers would enroll them in Little Leagues and coach them, so I gleaned from them. Internally, I wished my dad was there, but I just channeled that hurt into doing it myself. This self-determination resulted in me having to be more dedicated than most and work harder. Between my friends and the local could-have-been-great, urban-legend ballers in the recreation centers, I learned to play and love the game.

This showed up in my middle school years while I was playing basketball for Hutcheson, one of three schools in South Arlington that boasted most of the best athletes in the city. We had talented players on the team that grew up playing basketball in some of the most competitive leagues for children and had the motivation and parental support to push them. My mom and my cousins pushed me, and I ended up becoming a starting wingman for the team.

The team experienced a lot of success each year and won city championships and tournaments, which finally gave me a sense of achievement. Me, Marc Desgraves, was now a winner, a champion, an overcomer.

However, my transition into high school sports would present some interesting challenges. I knew I was good at basketball, but now I would have to compete with other talented and more highly recruited players. Sam Houston High School was a state powerhouse in basketball, football, and track. So despite my winning records at my previous school, I had to prove myself again and work my way into a role on the basketball team.

Eventually, I won a spot on the starting five that experienced a lot of success. As I look back, although I feel as if I didn't have much guidance or was lacking something, perhaps I was discovering something in myself that motivated me to push myself beyond limitations. This would show up again later in my college and professional years as well.

For the Love of Money

In between school and basketball, I worked my first job as a sacker at a local grocery store. I didn't save much of my money because I wanted to buy the type of name-brand clothes my mother couldn't afford. It took a lot of patience, kindness, and humility to make good tip money.

I wish I would have shown those traits on my second job at the local amusement park, but I was caught stealing cash at the shaved ice stand. I worked for ten to twelve hours each shift, with one thirty-minute break, in heat that often reached 100 degrees. I rationalized in my mind that the money stolen helped to balance out the perceived inequity of working in the blazing heat without many breaks. The run-in with amusement park law enforcement scared me and helped me learn self-discipline.

I never had a problem with hard work. Whether at my jobs as a teen or even later in life, I knew the value of work. I believe the Scripture is true and literal that says, "If you don't work, then you don't eat!" I would encourage young people today who struggle with always having to prove themselves or even despise all the chores that their parents make them do at home not to complain about it. That work—washing dishes, cutting grass, taking out the trash, and doing homework—teaches you the value of hard work and makes you develop a work ethic that will help you rise to the top later.

In becoming a professional, I've learned that nothing in life is given to you easily. If you want something in life or you want a better life, then you're going to have to outwork the next person. Being lazy in life won't get you anywhere.

However, my newfound self-discipline didn't include sex. I lost my virginity around the time I entered high school. By this time, instead of reaching out to my father or another trusted male figure, I was seeking guidance from my cousins, which was easier because my mother's sister and her three children, as well as my mother's youngest sister, were now living with us. My entire time in high school was spent living in a three-bedroom, two-bathroom house with eight people; and I slept in the living room alongside my two male cousins.

Stomp the Yard

I didn't do much dreaming or planning for life after high school. Looking back, I wish I had had my father to help me. My decision to attend Alabama State University was rushed and unplanned; and when I arrived on campus in August 1993, I didn't have any idea of what I wanted to major in. I was also homesick after just one week. I now know that a frequent saying is true: Nothing prepares you for real life like a HBCU.

From day one, I encountered challenges. Because I chose to attend ASU at the last minute, when I arrived there wasn't adequate housing to accommodate the influx of students.

When everyone else found which dormitories they would live in, I was told that I would have to live in a motel on the other side of town and would be bused back and forth to campus.

This motel wasn't the Ritz Carlton by any means. At night it was common to see guys selling drugs and prostitutes looking for their next trick just down the street from where I was staying. Living there also meant I had to get up earlier than students staying on campus so I could catch the bus or drive my car (which we called The Brown Hornet—a whole other story of its own).

> When people say, "The struggle is real," they are singing the theme song for my freshman year.

Although the accommodations were less than ideal, I had other worries. Since I didn't purchase a meal plan, I had to pay for my own meals and buy gas, which was a struggle because I didn't have a job or scholarship funds to depend on.

Then there were my battles with the financial aid department, an antiquated course-selection system, and my attempt to live with people who weren't friendly or who didn't appreciate good hygiene. When people say, "The struggle is real," they are singing the theme song for my freshman year.

Needless to say, my early days at ASU weren't shaping up to be the best experience.

Despite my early struggles, it wasn't long before my friends from back home and I met our second family. These guys were from Talladega, Alabama, and about ten of us instantly became friends our freshmen year. This group became my support system, my motivation, and my guidance in making decisions related to college.

The TallaDallas crew knew how to party and was smart enough to realize fairly quickly that partying could generate income if done right. Our friendship, hard work, and brand name grew stronger over time, and that wasn't by happenstance. Other students not only recognized our crew because of the parties we threw, but they also knew us for our performance in the classroom, where we all seemed to excel.

During this time, I quickly realized I couldn't figure things out on my own as I thought I could do in my high school years. I needed the support system of TallaDallas. I placed much more value on being prepared for class and being accountable as a student and as a friend to my brethren from TallaDallas. I studied harder and became a better test-taker and a group contributor in classes. My confidence level socially and academically was definitely boosted as my time on the yard and bond with TallaDallas grew.

It wasn't until later in life that I realized the full value of my TallaDallas relationship. As young men, we had similar goals and values, and this alignment has proven and will continue to prove to be invaluable for years to come.

Although I didn't know what to major in, the relationships with TallaDallas helped inspire me to dream big. President Theodore Roosevelt said, "The most important single ingredient in the formula of success is knowing how to get along with people." My ability to get along with others has always helped fill in the gaps in areas where I was lacking. For good or bad, I learned a lot about life by building relationships with others.

One of the best pieces of advice about life I could give would be to value relationships. Surround yourself with people who are like-minded and going in the same direction as you are. A leadership guru once said he could tell a lot about a person's future by looking at his or her phone call log. One of the key principles TDI teaches to our mentees is to understand and value important relationships because they can be the catalyst that inspires you to success or the ankle weight that brings you down to the bottom.

However, despite the brotherhood I formed with TallaDallas, I still had to work hard. Some of them were on presidential scholarships, had parents sending them money whenever they needed it, and seemed to have clearer direction initially. But as I began to discover what I wanted out of life, I found another internal motivation to excel. Despite the early challenges I faced at ASU, I began to put in late nights in the library, joined organizations on campus to help sharpen my leadership skills, and did whatever it took to excel.

One night, while in the library with Terrence Hall, I met a young lady who would one day become my wife and the mother of my children. Terrence, along with a few other friends, was part of the school's honor program. These guys would talk about different girls in the program and how cute they were. A few times I would see this young lady, but I didn't have the courage to approach her. But all things aligned one night when she came to the library. She was with a friend who was preparing for a test with Terrence. This was my chance, and I took it. She and I talked, and I immediately felt something toward her, even though we were involved in other relationships at the moment. After months of talking and becoming friends, we eventually became a couple, and the rest is history.

Adulthood

With hard work and sacrifice, I graduated at the top of my class with a degree in accounting; but it was life after college where I needed the most guidance. Unlike my grandfather and my father, I didn't want to replicate the bad DNA when it was my turn to be a father.

Part of my preparation for fatherhood centered around getting my career off on a solid foundation as an entry-level accountant at the local, but stable and conservative, utility company—boring to say the least. Without much time for development, reflection, and reaction, I enrolled in graduate school only a few semesters removed from ASU, which was too much to manage. I also became a certified public accountant during this time.

I thought I had life all figured out. I believed that a good foundation for fatherhood required that I get a good job, a new car, a new house, and a wife. In my mind, I was now living the American dream. I was married only one year out of college, and I became a father in 2001. In addition, the extra hours and sacrifice put in to advance quickly in my career and become a leader in and out of the office afforded me the opportunity to gain influence in many social circles and prepared me for what I thought was best for me.

However, in reality, it meant working too much and not giving all I could to my family. After college it takes time to learn and discover what makes you happy and where to direct your career path. Despite experiencing success right after college, I still had a lot to learn.

I know I am not alone in my story of growing up without a father's involvement or guidance. Hopefully, through my story you can learn the valuable lessons that I am still learning today.

Robert E. Quinn said, "That which you or I think is most unique about ourselves we hide. In ordinary discourse, in the normal state, we share our common self, our superficial self. Yet what is most unique about us is what has the greatest potential for bonding us. When we share our uniqueness, we discover the commonality in greatness that defines everyone on the planet."

Wherever I am invited to speak or participate in the TDI DREAMS Seminars we present in high schools, colleges, and community groups, I am discovering that most people aren't so different and that we all share similar experiences. Some people may look at my life and think it's all well because of my degrees, my status as a corporate vice president, and my

I know I am not alone in my story of growing up without a father's involvement or guidance.

beautiful family; but it hasn't been easy, and I had to work hard for everything. Despite my family DNA and the struggles I've had to overcome, I can say it's been worth it. However, I can also say that I'm just now identifying what my real dreams are, and the best is yet to come!

CHAPTER FIVE

BIRTHDAYS WERE THE WORST DAYS

TYRISH GARRETT

In 1972, the Dallas Cowboys won Super Bowl VI, the Los Angeles Lakers won the NBA Finals, HBO was launched by Time Warner, Bill Withers' "Lean On Me" was a number one hit, and the United Negro College Fund slogan "A mind is a terrible thing to waste" was created. The summer of 1972 was also the year of my conception. It was a conception that almost didn't make it to full term.

On an unusually warm 71-degree day, gunshots rang out a couple of blocks away from my mother's home. By the end of the day, one person was dead, and two were injured. A state trooper was killed, and one policeman was wounded.

Some 30 officers responded to the scene where the suspect took refuge in a basement, and a shootout ensued. The suspect was shot more than 20 times before being flushed from the basement with tear gas. Authorities later identified the assailant as 22-year-old Howard Leonard, my father. He was transferred to a local Birmingham hospital where he was listed in critical condition.

Why did one person end up dead and two injured? It started during the Vietnam War. My father was a SPC4 in the United States Army. After he came back from Vietnam, his mental state started to change. What would make a man carry a rifle while naked from one side of town to the other? As it turns out, my father was on his way to shoot my mother and kill me that December day. His mental state was in such disarray that he thought I would be born a white baby and I had to be killed. Fortunately, my father survived his wounds. Through mental and physical rehab, my father's mental state returned to normal. However, he ended up paralyzed from the waist down.

My father was on his way to shoot my mother and kill me.

On March 1, 1973, I was born Tyrish Derell Garrett, son of Howard Leonard and Brenda Garrett. I was a typical child growing up. I grew up in a household with my immediate family (Grandma, two uncles, an aunt, and a cousin). As most grandmothers do, my grandmother gave me the freedom and opportunity to do whatever I wanted to do. If my mother, aunt, or uncles went somewhere and I wanted to go, I went. It did not matter if they went to the grocery store (A&P), Woolworth, or even the liquor store, I went and no one said a thing.

My grandmother, Julia Garrett, was a strong, independent woman. As one story goes, she dragged her sister's husband out of another woman's house and whipped him in the process. My grandmother was also responsible for my nickname—Peter Red—and I would venture to say most people in Talladega do not know my real name.

At age two, I was a fat kid walking around in overalls. Back then they referred to you as "husky." I was always into something, whether it was stealing bubblegum from A&P or getting into things I should not have. However, one evening that behavior caught up with me.

My mother and I were at a friend's apartment when I slipped into a bedroom. I climbed a dresser and opened a bottle of medicine. I took several pills and staggered back into the living room. Everyone realized something was wrong and that I had taken several pills. I was rushed to the hospital and treated. The doctor told my family that I needed to stay awake for the next 12 hours. According to my aunt, they had everyone in the neighborhood come to our house to play with me. Suffice it to say, everything turned out OK.

I often get asked how I got the scar on my face. People assume that I got cut or was in a fight, but the real reason is not quite so sinister. As a kid, I was always into something. One day, I was riding my rocking horse on the front porch. Back then, porches had a low end and a high end, and you can imagine which end I was riding on. As I rocked back and forth, each time with more intensity, I bounced higher and higher, so much so that the rocking horse's tail hit the porch. When that happened, I flipped forward off the porch and landed on my face. I didn't land on any glass or rocks; but because I was so fat, my face just split.

Unfortunately, the attending doctor did a bad job stitching up my face. I can still count the holes where I had stitches. Over the years, I've often thought about having the scar removed, but I don't because it is a constant reminder of the young, adventurous boy I once was.

IT WAS ALL A DREAM

Potential at an Early Age

In 1978, I attended Westside Head Start. That was where I discovered my love for academics and athletics. I remember sitting in the classroom and being able to answer most questions and solve many problems without much assistance. My teacher, Mrs. Scott, said that I would be good in sports. I was ultra-competitive during P.E., and I particularly excelled at baseball. Academics and athletics had begun to shape who I would become later in life.

Later that same year, my brother, Brian, was born; and one of the first things my grandmother told my mother was that she wasn't to treat me any differently after my brother was born. However, after being the only child for so long, I had grown accustomed to all of the attention. Brian was a quiet baby. He didn't cry much, and he was easy to care for, so I'm not sure why one day I decided to put a pillow over his head. Even as my mother found me smothering Brian, with his legs kicking violently, he still did not cry. I guess at that age I wanted all the attention I could get.

In 1979, I started elementary school and began to excel academically. I found that class work and homework were not that difficult for me, and I was able to complete my work with minimal help. I was one of the top students in my class. However, one day I got my first taste of accountability. My teacher sent a note home to my mother. Little did I know that the note accused me of stealing a fellow student's Hot Wheels car. After a little back and forth, I confessed, and there were repercussions for the theft. The car was returned the next day.

My evenings after school and during the summer were spent on the baseball field. My friends and I spent hours every day playing baseball, tag, racing, and football. One day during that summer, I was playing football with two other friends and was tackled. As I got up, I was tackled again, and a sharp pain went through my right arm. I walked across the street to the house and complained about my arm. I was told to put some ice on it.

The next morning, I woke up complaining, and my mother took me to the doctor. My arm was broken just above the elbow. I had to wear a rigid cast for six weeks. In terms of playing with friends, my broken arm was just a minor setback. Once healed, I continued to play sports. The amount of time we spent on the baseball field honed our skills for all types of athletics. As the years passed, the kids in my neighborhood were so competitive in baseball that girls sometimes were chosen over some of the guys.

Eye-Opening Experiences

By the fall of 1982, I continued to excel academically and athletically. I continued to get A's and B's, and I would be so excited about my good report cards that I would run home to show my family what I had achieved. Once I had shown my report card to my family; I would dash out the back door and run over to Mrs. Graham's house so she could see my accomplishments.

Just like clockwork Mrs. Graham—or Honeypie, as she was known—would bake me a pound cake. She told me from the time I started school that if I made the A&B Honor Roll, she would bake me a cake every six weeks. Up till this point, I cannot ever remember not receiving a cake.

During the summer of 1981, my uncle, Willie J. Garrett, took me, along with one of his friends, to an Atlanta Braves games. To say this was the highlight of my life is an understatement. Before going to that game, I had never been outside my hometown. I hounded my uncle all morning about what time we were leaving. The game wasn't until four o'clock that evening. The Braves played the Cincinnati Reds and lost 9-1. However, Dale Murphy hit a homerun that day. I can't remember how many Braves games I have watched since that day.

It was around this time I would read and look at pictures of different places in the set of encyclopedias my family had. I learned a lot about history, animals, and even human anatomy. Many of you probably remember those glossy pictures of human bodies in the encyclopedia. I used those books to travel in my mind all over the United States and around the world.

Academically and athletically, my fifth-grade year was good until I decided to become a follower. I joined a group of students bullying another student in P.E., and I ended up slapping him. After being sent to the office, I was made to sit out a week from P.E. The punishment was devastating to me because I realized that I had allowed someone to influence the decisions I made, and I felt bad for slapping a fellow classmate.

My P.E. teacher sat me down and had a profound conversation with me. She talked to me about the decisions I had made, as well as the consequences for my actions. Each year, she gave out various awards at an assembly of the entire student body. My focus had been on receiving the award for Best All Around (academics and athletics) and Best Athlete.

During our conversation, she informed me that I would not win any awards because of my actions.

On the day of the awards ceremony, after sitting through a rather lengthy program, my name was called for first runner-up for Best Athlete. I received a blue ribbon but not the trophy. Despite the conversation with my teacher, I was still devastated. Shortly after the ceremony, my P.E. teacher explained to me that she could not give me the trophy for Best Athlete based on my actions. That was a lesson I would never forget.

In 1984, I played organized baseball for the first time. The game of baseball came easy to me, as I could play every position except catcher. However, off the field was a little more difficult. The first or second day of practice, I took a note to my coach asking to be traded to another team that one of my friends played on. I could see the look on my coach's face.

I asked for a trade because my family did not have a car. Every day, I rode my bike approximately five miles one-way to practice. Another challenge for me was that our games were played at night. After some thought, the coach decided to give me a ride on game days. To the coach's credit, although he lived only a quarter of a mile from the field, he would drive across town to pick me up and take me home after the game.

We had a good season and were 13-2. We lost to the same team twice. I batted third or fourth during the season and pitched or played shortstop. After a great season, there was still a void in my life. First, after all of my accomplishments during that season, none of my family attended any of my games, a theme that would play out for the rest of my athletic life. Second,

I did not make the 11-year-old all-star team. Talk about being disappointed. I was good enough to make the 12-year-old team.

Several people told me that no one knew my name since it was my first year playing, but years later I realized why I didn't make the team—daddy ball. Daddy ball is when a father coaches a team so his son can occupy a choice position on the team and have more playing time. However, despite this setback, I would make the all-star team for the next four years.

During the 1984–1985 school year, the board of education decided to make changes regarding classification. They moved the fifth grade to elementary school and the sixth grade to middle school. The changes placed my class back at Dixon Middle School and with our teachers from the previous year. As luck would have it, I had my P.E. teacher from the year before when I missed out on the coveted Best All Around award, but this year I was ready.

I earned A&B Honor Roll every six weeks. I won the singles and doubles trophy in tennis, I won the doubles trophy in Ping-Pong, and I finished second in singles Ping-Pong. On awards day, after sitting through another lengthy ceremony, my name was called for the final and most prestigious award. I won Best All Around (academics and athletics) performance. It was the proudest moment of my young life.

The 1985 Little League season was dramatically different. My team went 2-13 that year, which made for a long season. In addition, I lost to all of my friends in the neighborhood because they were on different teams. That year I was on the 12-year-old team, and I still faced disappointments. We played our first game in Sylacauga, and it was the first time I ever rode the bench in baseball or football. I almost cried, but I kept telling myself I would get in the next inning. The next inning never came, and we lost 9-1 in a double elimination tournament.

I have to give the assistant coach credit because he made several changes prior to the next game, and I started in left field and batted sixth. That was the last time I ever rode the bench on an all-star team. By the time the tournament was over, I was batting third or fourth, depending on the lineup.

We won the county tournament and the regional. Then we played in the state tournament in Florence, Alabama. This game took me on the second major trip I had ever taken. We were at the tournament for almost a week and finished at 2-2. At that time, that was a major accomplishment because we were the first team from Talladega to win two games in the state tournament. Our banner still hangs in the Spring Street Recreational Center.

Growing up, we didn't have a lot; but my family did provide us with video games and bikes. However, 1986 was a tough summer for me. All of my friends had a moped or Honda Spree, and it was hard for me to keep up with them on a bicycle.

We would gather at one of our houses that morning, and then they would head out for what seemed like all day. I would ride my bike in the neighborhood or play video games. I didn't understand why my family couldn't afford to buy me a moped, so being left behind by my friends was a tough pill to swallow. Every once in a while, someone would double me, but it was hard for that person to keep up with the pack, so I didn't get to double very often.

That summer, I overheard someone say something disturbing about me. A man told my aunt's boyfriend, "That little ni**r ain't gonna be shit unless he plays baseball." Can you imagine telling that to a 13-year-old child? That quote has stuck with me until this day. As a child, I knew I always wanted to achieve something beyond my neighborhood. Funny enough, from that point on I used that quote as one of many motivating factors to push me to achieve.

Where, How, and Who Do I Fit in With?

I reached my high school freshman year in 1987. Like so many freshmen do coming from middle school to high school, I discovered that I was definitely out of my league. Fitting in socially with the upperclassmen was the biggest challenge. As a typical freshman, I wanted to belong, so as I had so often done before, I focused on academics and athletics.

As a junior, I made the B-team basketball team. I was a decent player, and I had one good game. Because the starters showed up late for warm-ups, I was able to start the game. The second string started out great; we were substituted for around the four-minute mark. When we left the game, we were up ten points, and I had scored ten points on five of five shooting. I was feeling it and was in my zone. The peculiar thing was that several back-ups, including myself, never got back in the game. We ended up losing by ten points.

Spring of 1990 was baseball season. I made the varsity team and was competing for the starting position at second base. Once again, I found myself in another daddy ball situation. For the starting position, I had to compete against the son of a bank vice-president. I found myself as the designated hitter for the first few games; and to add insult to injury, I was batting ninth. I was perplexed as the designated hitter and not playing in the field. I knew the guy I was competing against wasn't better than I was.

After a few games, I was batting seventh, then sixth, and then leadoff. I was also playing in left field as an everyday player. I guess it was difficult to justify keeping a .393 hitter and school walks leader on the bench.

Our team had a great season, and we made it to the quarterfinals of the state tournament. That season, the Talladega High School team advanced further than any other team from our school had done in the past. However, we lost a heartbreaker at home, 10-7.

That summer brought me ever closer to graduation. I was starting to think more about college and how I would pay for it. I signed up for an eight-year commitment (six years active, two years inactive) with the Army Reserves as a way to help pay for my college tuition. I was able to sit out the first year because I was still in high school, and that year counted toward my active status.

As the school year continued, I stayed on task with my academics and had passed all of the standardized tests. Now the question was where I planned to attend college. My guidance counselor had given me only minimal attention. One teacher even told me that I should attend a community college, which I considered an insult considering I had one of the highest, if not the highest, test average in her class. I had a few pamphlets and financial aid papers to review and complete, and that fall I decided to skip playing basketball to focus on school and baseball.

The 1991 baseball season kicked off, and there was no doubt about me starting. I was back at my natural position (second base) and batting lead-off. The year was going great; we were winning and playing good ball. Then one day, two of my teammates and I went to the coach's office and saw a note to a college coach. The note discussed the attributes of our high school coach's son and how great he was. This didn't sit well with any of us.

Although we were the team's lead-off and third and fourth batters, none of us had received any scholarship offers or had had any discussions with our coach about playing baseball after high school. Our high school baseball team had been to the playoffs every year since I was in eighth grade. We had enough talent on some of our teams to play in the minor leagues, so much so that there was a professional scout following our team, which leads me to believe there were college scouts following us as well.

Eventually, I talked with my coach and committed to play baseball at Alabama State University. I was having a great year athletically and personally. I had a girlfriend, and everything was going well. Then all of a sudden, I decided to dump my girlfriend. Thinking back on it, it was just teenage immaturity at its finest. The sad part about it was I chose to break things off two weeks before the prom. She was heartbroken. I still cringe when I think about it today.

On the day of the prom, the team had its final regular season game. We played Dadeville, and I had one of the best games of my life. I struck out my first at bat, and I looked at the catcher and said to myself, *Your pitcher is in trouble*. My next at bat was a solo homerun over the left field wall. My third at bat was a deep drive to center field. I was in my homerun trot until the ball hit off the 17-foot wall. I ended up with a triple. My fourth at bat was another solo homerun over the left field wall. By this time, little kids were hanging around the dugout asking questions and wanting to talk. I was on top of the world.

During my fifth at bat, I felt great. Swing and a miss, strike one. I swung at strike two, and my shoulder popped out of place. I couldn't even finish the at bat. Coach sent someone in to finish the at bat, and they swung and missed. It counted as a strikeout against me because I started the at bat. We won the game and headed home for prom night.

To go to prom in style, I had borrowed a car from a friend of mine. It was a candy-apple red I-ROC Z, and it was clean. I brought along a bottle of wine for later. I picked up my date. She looked good, and I was feeling good in my all-white tux, white gloves, gold bow tie, and a matching gold cummerbund. Everything was going well, and we were having a good time until the DJ announced that the driver of a red I-ROC Z should step outside.

Outside, I was met by a police officer who wanted me to take out the brown bag that was partially tucked under the driver's seat of my borrowed car. The bag contained my bottle of wine. The officer reminded me that I was underage and that prom night was an important night. He told me that if I wanted the wine back, my parents could come to the station and pick it up. That bottle never made it back to the station, and I was just thankful the officer was in a good mood. All in all, it was a good night.

The end of May 1991 marked my graduation. Even though graduation was not until the end of the month, Donta Truss and I spent the two weeks before school ended partying and hanging out. Neither of us had to take graduation exams or final exams. We spent those two weeks hanging out with two girls in our class.

On graduation night, it was party time. Mrs. Honeypie, Erica Graham's grandmother, gave her the biggest graduation party I had ever attended. Cars were parked several blocks away. There were students everywhere; and there was plenty food, music, and fun.

Exposure 2.0 (Never Going Home)

On July 3, I reported to the Air Force Base in Montgomery, headed to Ft. Sill, Oklahoma, for basic training. My job was 13 Bravo (Field Artillery). This was the first time I had ever flown on a plane. I flew from Alabama to Texas and then on to Oklahoma. Then I took another flight from Oklahoma City to Ft. Sill on a crop duster that bounced around. As soon as the wheels touched down at Ft. Sill, I grabbed the airsickness bag, but I still considered it a successful flight.

The first two or three days in basic training provided a little bit of culture shock for me. A guy from Birmingham came over to my bunk and told me that if I wanted to go AWOL he would go with me. At the time, we didn't understand we were in processing and had not made it to our final destination. The next two weeks would be totally different—two weeks of straight hell!

During that time, we had no telephone, letters, newspapers, sweets, or any of the comforts of home; and we didn't have a clue about what was going on in the outside world. I watched one guy struggle to perform 15 pull-ups and 15 push-ups in two minutes. Overall, the training wasn't easy, but I was in decent shape before I got there. I actually gained 15 pounds over the 13-week period. However, I saw several guys lose a third to half of their body weight.

During those first nine weeks of training, I had my first experience shooting an M16, M203 Grenade Launcher and a 50-caliber machine gun. I also had the pleasure of experiencing Oklahoma's extreme weather. Some days the temperature would exceed 120 degrees, while some nights the temperatures fell below freezing.

One of my most memorable moments was the 20-mile hike during week nine. We left at approximately 9:00 P.M. with more than 50 pounds of gear and our M16. We reached our barracks at approximately 5:00 A.M. Some guys dropped out with approximately three or four miles left. They had to repeat the 20 miles before they would be allowed to pass the course.

Once I could see the barracks, all I could think about was lying down to rest, but our drill sergeants had a different plan. We sat in a field across from the barracks and ate breakfast. It didn't help that it was cold, and the dew fell on us as we sat out there. The remaining four weeks were not as difficult. We were in class most of the day learning our respective MOS (job).

When graduation day arrived, we were all ready to go home, but basic training would not be what it was without one last setback.

Our Sergeant Major told four of us that the bus would pick us up at 1:00 P.M. to go to the airport. The bus actually came at noon.

Three of us decided we would take a cab to Oklahoma City to catch our plane, which cost us $137; but at this point, money was no object to get home. The fourth person decided he would go back to the barracks and wait for the next bus, but the next bus never came. He was able to convince the Sergeant Major to give him a ride to the airport. He made it just as we were boarding.

After basic training, I spent the rest of the year preparing to attend Alabama State University. Although my good friend Donta had planned to attend Talladega College, I convinced him to go to State with me. However, he stretched his decision out until the first of January, waiting for me to change my mind.

We arrived on campus and had no idea where we were supposed to be and what we were supposed to do. Fortunately, we met Daryl (Ambassador), and he took us to the places we needed to go and to people we needed to see. Being from a small town, Donta and I were distracted by being in a larger city, by girls, by malls, and anything else that caught our eyes. To make matters worse, we did not realize that only freshmen reported to school a week earlier. During our first week at ASU, we naively thought we were running things on campus. When the upperclassmen reported a few days later, we quickly realized what it actually meant to be a freshman.

I was assigned to the second floor of Benson Hall since I was going to play baseball. One of my roommates was from Chicago, and the other one was from Detroit. The roommate from Detroit was Muslim. That was the first time I had met someone who practiced Islam. One of the first times I saw him practicing his faith was around lunchtime. I burst into our dorm room, and he and three other Muslims were in the middle of the floor praying toward the East. I quietly stepped out of the room and waited about ten minutes until they were finished.

Two weeks into the semester, a professor called out a list of names and told those students to stand. I had no clue what he was about to ask. The professor told those standing that we could not return to class until our financial debt had been cleared. My invoice balance was about $370. I knew there was no way I could come up with that much money, and calling home was not an option. Someone recommended that I talk with the financial aid director. I met with Mr. Billy Brooks, and he asked, "What was your GPA in high school?" I told him it was 3.30. He gave me $500 in financial aid and told me to go back to class. Mr. Brooks is one name I will never forget.

> **He gave me $500 in financial aid and told me to go back to class.**

The rest of the semester was a breeze. That fall, I decided to move off campus with Donta. We lived in a two-bedroom, single-wide trailer on Troy Highway. It was so tiny that Donta's full-size bed took up his whole room. At that time, I didn't have a car or a job. Fortunately, Donta allowed me to drive his car, and I soon got a job at Jeans West in Eastdale Mall, which was convenient because Donta worked at Kenny's Shoes.

Then, we moved to The Seasons Apartments, which was a significant step up, but I was still struggling. Rent at The

Seasons was a little higher, and I still didn't have a car. I had to fit my schedule around Donta's schedule, and there were some days I missed class because I didn't have a ride.

One day, I ran into Chris Garrett, a good friend of mine I have known since third grade. I talked with him, and he told me he drove back and forth from Talladega to Montgomery every day. In exchange for the use of his car, I promised him he could stay with us rent-free until he got himself settled. So Chris moved in and soon got a job at Morrison's in Eastdale Mall. Being able to use Chris's car made it a little easier for me to get to class, but we still struggled to make ends meet. Sometimes, it was difficult to eat once a day, and even then our meals consisted of rice and chicken backs. Believe me, there's not much meat on a chicken back.

With spring came the Blizzard of '93, and we were not prepared. The snowstorm dropped at least a foot of snow on Montgomery. With no food, no electricity, and only the blankets we had on our beds, those were a rough couple of days. By the end of the year, our friendship had hit a snag. The three of us were supposed to move into a three-bedroom apartment on the other side of the complex, but Chris and I had a disagreement with Donta and moved out.

In January, things started looking up for me. I got my income tax refund. With that and a few dollars I had saved, I went to an auto auction in Gadsden. I drove home in a 1984 Honda Prelude. I now had the freedom to go where I pleased, but my grades had begun to slip. We also needed a third roommate for the apartment.

In March, Gerald Blakely, my assistant manager at work, expressed an interest in moving in with us. I told Gerald that if he moved in, I would pay his first month's rent. A week or so later, he took me up on my offer. In the beginning, our arrangement worked out all right, but as time went on, it got progressively worse. Not only was Gerald lacking in good personal hygiene, but he caused us other concerns as well. He left dishes in the sink, food on the floor, and various other items out in the open. He was not keen on paying his rent and other bills on time.

Our power bill had gotten significantly behind, and one day there was a knock at the door. It was Alabama Power. The man asked if I had the money to pay, and I said no. He said, "Cut them," and I said yes. I promptly called Gerald and explained what had happened. To cover the cost of having our power turned back on, I made him pawn some of his possessions.

However, the final straw came when Chris's parents gave him a trash bag full of meat for us to stock the freezer. I had been away on reserve duty; and as I drove into our apartment complex, I noticed a party in progress. I also realized that someone was barbecuing. I asked Gerald what was up, and he told me he had had a few friends over and had put some meat on the grill. Chris and I were livid! Without asking, Gerald had taken the meat given to Chris and used it to host a barbecue.

That fall, Jeremy Spratling moved in with us. My personal and academic struggles continued. We didn't have enough money, so we were barely eating, and I invested in a pair of clippers and rubber bands and started cutting my own hair. (I used the rubber band to get an even line around my head so I could fade it in.) I couldn't take it any more. I told Jeremy and Chris I would be moving back to campus in the spring. I wanted to give them ample time to find a place to live. We also told Gerald we would be moving out soon. Then he rode back by the apartment on moving day to see if we were actually moving.

In the spring of 1995, I moved to the New Dunn Tower on campus. Things started to pick up right away. It was as if I had caught my second wind. My grades were improving since I didn't have the stress of paying bills or have to worry about my next meal. Unfortunately, the cafeteria food was not that great. I had gotten a breather and an opportunity to gather myself. Spring break was exactly what I needed. I experienced my first Freaknic in Atlanta. I had never seen that many people in one setting. We spent two days partying in downtown Atlanta.

I only needed one semester back on campus to get back on track. That summer, I moved into Bridgecroft Apartments with Chris and Jeremy. A few months later, we moved into a three-bedroom apartment at Eastdale Apartments. I got a new job at Blockbuster on Atlanta Highway, which was in walking distance from our new place.

Shortly after the move, Chris had a son, and his girlfriend, Wendy, moved in, which was a significant change for all of us. Although we tried to act as if nothing had changed, we would take Jacolby, our snake, on campus with us. It was all good until Wendy saw us talking to a couple of ladies with Jacolby in hand. I think that was the last time we took Jacolby on campus.

That fall and the following spring brought a significant academic challenge. I was taking all major course work.

Dean Vaughn walked into our management class and told us he wanted a ten-page paper from everyone because we were having too much fun while the instructor was out of the class. Little did we know that this would become the standard for the College of Business Administration (COBA) going forward. For every COBA course, we were required to write a ten-page paper. Combined with the advanced course, my late nights in the computer lab began. The computer lab was open 24 hours a day, and nights I was there until the wee hours of the morning.

By spring, I was able to have some much-needed down time. My friends and I made our first spring break trip to Daytona. We left at midnight Thursday night and arrived in Daytona around 7:30 A.M. It was amazing to see that many people at the beach, but strangely enough, no one was in the water. It didn't matter to us, though. We had 72 hours of straight partying.

By the summer of 1996, I could see the finish line. I only had five courses left to take. I took two that summer and three in the fall, so I was no longer a full-time student. I scored well in all of my fall classes; but my marketing class, taught by Dean Vaughn, presented another challenge. Dean Vaughn decided at the end of the year to give every student an incomplete grade. I talked to him about the incomplete grade and told him this was my last class before I graduated. He dismissed me as only he could. It bothered me for a little while; and then I thought, *I can't graduate until spring anyway.*

Throughout the spring, I continued to plead my case, but Dean Vaughn told me I needed to do more but wouldn't tell me exactly what that meant. A week before graduation, I still had a grade of incomplete. I was beginning to have doubts as to whether I would graduate. I talked with the dean one last time, and he changed my grade to a C. Actually, I deserved an A, but I decided that at that point it wasn't going to matter.

With no questions asked, he gave me the money.

Before I could relax, however, I faced another hurdle. ASU claimed that I owed $480, and it had to be paid before I could graduate. I had no idea where I would get that kind of money on such short notice. I finally called my father and explained to him that I needed $500 in order to graduate. With no questions asked, he gave me the money.

Finally, Graduation Day 1997 arrived. Receiving that degree was the greatest accomplishment of my life. The expectation of my neighborhood in Talladega, my friends, and my family were finally realized.

Real World

That summer, I started working in the collections department at Regions Bank. I learned valuable information about obtaining loans, contractual obligation of loans, and what banks can do to access customer's accounts. One of the funniest things to happen while I was working at the bank occurred when my next-door neighbor bought a car through a straw purchase. A straw purchase is when someone buys a vehicle for another person without the intent of paying the loan. My neighbor's car payment was significantly past due, and I told her roommate to talk to her about it. That Friday night, I went to a party at their apartment. We were having a good time, but I reminded the roommate to talk with the car owner about her late payment. Monday morning, Jeremy and I knocked on our neighbor's door. I let Jeremy take the lead because the smile on my face was too big. Jeremy told her to remove her personal belongings from the vehicle and hand over the keys. After a little haggling with her, I drove the car to the bank. The following weekend, we were back at her apartment partying, but she never said a word about the repossessed vehicle!

One day, I went to lunch in the cafeteria at work and saw this beautiful woman, dressed all in black, walking by. Based on the person she was having lunch with, I knew she worked in customer service. I made a few calls to get more information and to plant a bug. After some time had passed, I happened to call the customer service center; and out of almost 100 customer service associates, Pallas, the intriguing, beautiful woman, answered my call. She had an idea who I was, but we had a nice conversation on company time and found out we had mutual interests. We talked so long that I forgot what I called about and had to call back later to get the information I needed.

A year later, the collections department was downsized, and I was moved to customer service—the worst job at the bank. After about nine months, I talked with my former boss and moved back to collections. After looking at my banking options, I decided to apply for graduate school at Troy State

University in Montgomery (TSUM). I enrolled in a 14-month program. While taking a full class load at TSUM, I was still working at Regions and also dating Pallas.

Then disaster struck. The used car I had just bought slung a rod. With my car down, I had no way to get to work or to school. Pallas lived up the street from Alabama State University, and I was living in Ski Lodge Apartments out in East Montgomery. Every day for at least six months, Pallas picked me up in the morning and we drove back downtown to work. After work she made sure I made it to class and then picked me up around 10:00 that night after class.

In the spring of 1999, I graduated from TSUM with an M.B.A in business administration. I also pledged Kappa Alpha Psi (KAY) and forged several valuable relationships.

The following year, the start of the new millennium, brought renewed excitement to my life. In January, I proposed to Pallas, and fortunately she said yes. Our wedding date was set for the last Saturday in October. As I thought about the date, I realized that was the same weekend as the Magic City Classic, so we moved the date to November 4. Marrying Pallas was the best thing to ever happen to me. Everything she has ever done for me has always been in my best interest. She is always positive and encouraging, and she provides the perfect balance for me.

In February, I had an interview at UPS in the finance department. The manager drove down from Birmingham to interview me. A month later, on my birthday, I was offered the position. I gave Regions my two-week notice and took the specialist position at UPS. I became the revenue auditor trainer for the state of Alabama and the Florida panhandle. After approximately a year at UPS, I was told it would be in my best interest to move to Birmingham to be near the district office.

In 2010, our son Kiian graduated high school and decided to attend the University of Alabama at Birmingham. The college experience was an eye-opener for him. It gave him an opportunity to experience new things and meet new people with different perspectives on life. Presently, Kiian is taking time to gather himself. He had too much fun and lost focus. We all take different paths to our destinations.

In 2013, I turned 40 years young. My wife planned a surprise birthday party for me. Jeremy and I hung out the night before, but I had no idea of the surprise awaiting me the next day. I was not feeling my best on my birthday so I lay in bed most of the day.

Pallas finally made me get up and put on a suit, which made me wonder just where we were going. I thought we might go to a nice restaurant, listen to some music, and spend the night downtown. She put me in the car and blindfolded me. When we arrived at our destination, Pallas took off the blindfold, and I saw family members and friends from Talladega I hadn't seen in years.

Pallas did a great job putting together a masquerade-themed birthday party, and the slide show was awesome. Growing up, I never traveled far from home; however, watching that video made me realize just how much of this country and some places abroad I have now visited. It only took 40 years, but this was my first ever birthday party.

CHAPTER SIX

SPREAD LOVE.
IT'S THE BROOKLYN WAY
TERRENCE HALL

The Formative Years

I was born on July 12, 1975, at Citizens Hospital in Talladega, Alabama, to proud parents Mark Boyd Hall and Jonnie Meryle Hall. My father was from Cincinnati, Ohio, and my mom was from Greenville, Alabama. He was a laborer, and she was an educator, so our family lived quite comfortably until my parents' divorce and infamous "Reaganomics" kicked in. I was five when my father left us, and I didn't see him again until I was 15 and a church trip took me to his hometown.

When my mom was laid off from her job, the financial woes began in earnest; but through a series of odd jobs and the support of my mother's parents, Cecil and Vicie Lewis, we always managed to have enough. Even when my younger brother, Kevin, came along a few years later, we never went without, whether it was food, clothes, shelter, and ordinances.

One anchor we could always count on in our lives was the presence of the Lord. My grandparents raised my mother and her siblings in church, missing church wasn't an option. My uncle, the Reverend Willie Joe Lewis, was the pastor of Rocky Mount Baptist Church, which was the church we attended. We may have had it hard, but having God in our lives and being surrounded by our loving and supportive family gave us a sense of love that would pave the way for my life and the people in it.

The Support System

Being active in the church also gave me another family— my church family. Then again, when you're in church three or four times a week like we were, church members do become almost like family. After my uncle passed away, I attended my grandparents' church, Greater Ebenezer Missionary Baptist Church. Under the guidance of the Reverend Dr. B. E. McKinney, our church family was like no other.

The older members were like uncles and aunts; and the younger members like brothers, sisters, and cousins. We participated together in church, district meetings, and statewide functions, as well as the choir, usher board, vacation Bible school, Sunbeams, Crusaders, and YWA programs. Needless to say, we spent quite a bit of time in church.

If we wanted to go to the skating rink Sunday night to meet up with our friends, we made it our business to go to church— rain, hail, sleet, or snow; for good or bad, in sickness, or in health. When our pastor had preaching engagements at other churches, he knew members of his congregation would be there to show him love and support.

There was no question that our pastor returned that love and support for us. When we needed someone to talk to, he was more than willing to listen and offer wise counsel. Rev. McKinney's pastoral love and guidance has stayed with me all of my life and has inspired me to offer that same type of love, care, and understanding to others.

Growing up I was taught the value of getting a good education. For the most part, I believe I've done rather well in honoring that. Of course, with my mother being an educator, I probably didn't have much of a choice. From elementary school forward, I was a pretty good student. I was always on the honor roll with mostly A's and a few B's from time to time.

As far as my social life in school, I tended to be the student other children wanted to be around. From an early age, I learned how to be a good friend. For example, during recess one day, the school administrators were trying to find one of my classmates. When they couldn't find her, my teacher said, "Just find Terry Hall, and I'm quite sure she will be close by," and it was true!

The Formation

During junior high school, I took accelerated courses; and in high school, I signed up for the advanced diploma curriculum. I enrolled in advanced placement courses and became a member of the National Honor Society, Mu Alpha Theta Math Honor Society, and the Student Government Association.

My senior year, I was elected president of the Class of 1993. I was the salutatorian of my class with a 4.02 grade point average. I received numerous scholarship offers from universities across the country, but I didn't want to travel too far from home. So I chose to attend Alabama State University in Montgomery, Alabama, on a Presidential

Scholarship that paid all of my expenses and even offered a stipend each semester.

I knew my mother didn't have much money; but because of the love she instilled in me and the sacrifices she made as a single parent, this was my way of thanking her and paying her back for all she had done. Several of my classmates and friends decided to attend ASU as well, and as friends we formed an unbreakable life-long bond.

#MyASU

I entered Alabama State University as a freshman in the fall of 1993, and I lived in William H. Benson Hall, Room 120. Living in Benson was an unforgettable experience. Until its demolition recently, I thought that every person who entered the hallowed halls of Bama State should have to spend at least one semester at Benson, just for the memories alone.

Going off to college was not my first time away from home, but it would be the first time I lived with a complete stranger. I said goodbye to my family and took that one and a half-hour trek down Highway 231. I checked into my dormitory and opened the door to see a guy sleeping under a Detroit Lions blanket. Why he was still asleep at 3:00 P.M. was beyond me. I guess the college life experience was already showing him a good time.

He woke up after he heard my key in the door. We exchanged pleasantries, and I found out he was Ramone Harper from Dallas/Arlington, Texas, by way of Detroit, Michigan. I had only been to Detroit once for a family reunion, and I'd never been to Texas, so I thought he and I wouldn't work out as roommates. (In fact, my friend Terrance was supposed to be my roommate, but somehow that got messed up in the paperwork—good ol' housing office at State!) However, Ramone and I would become the greatest of friends and as close as brothers. We would become the common ground that formed the great TallaDallas brotherhood.

That would come later. In the meantime, as I settled into my dorm room and campus life, I could only wonder then if Ramone and I would be good roommates. I consoled myself by thinking that there were at least ten other guys from back home attending ASU, so I wouldn't lack for friendship.

Later that day, I found my Talladega friends, and we had dinner and just talked about this new life we were about to embark on; but we also knew that we would have to look out for one another even more. We talked about our new roommates, the dorm conditions, and the girls on campus. The consensus was that we were in our element—no more parents and no more curfews. We were free to do what we wanted to do. Yeah, we were gonna love this!

Although I was away from home, some of my cousins lived in Montgomery, so my sense of family would be intact. However, I knew I had to form some kind of kinship with my roommate, Ramone, because we would be living together for the next few months at least.

As Ramone and I became better acquainted, I discovered that there were two other guys from Texas at ASU. I met Marc and Scott and introduced them to my crew from home. We all got along so well that we started hanging out together. During one of the first weekends at school, we ran into one another at a local nightclub. We talked and enjoyed the music and seemed drawn together. After experiencing the nightlife, we became genuine friends and began to cement the bonds of our brotherhood.

We ate together, took classes together, studied together, attended football and basketball games together, played intramural basketball together, and bonded together. We even had a set ritual every afternoon. We would all come back to my dorm room and watch old episodes of the sitcom *Martin* on the VCR and play spades. The fun we had in Room 120 nourished our friendships and will be with us forever.

The social gatherings were of epic proportions.

My cousin lived within walking distance of campus, so our group would gather at his house. These social gatherings were of epic proportions. Along with our group were other students we invited, and these gatherings were the beginning of our party life, which would become our signature.

Toward the end of our first semester, most people came to realize the if you saw one of us you would more than likely see another one because we were always together. Before we went home for Christmas, we threw a party for one another to celebrate finishing our first semester of college and the beginning of our newly formed friendship.

The Transition

The next few semesters only served to strengthen our bond. By this time, our brotherhood was solid. Unfortunately, some of the original crew didn't return to school; but the core group remained intact, and we eventually took on a few students who were older than us.

After a few more of the social gatherings we had become known for, we decided to increase our campus presence, which was around the time we came up with our name, TallaDallas, a play on our hometowns of Talladega and Dallas. As part of our signature look, we wore our red Texas Rangers caps.

Over time, we improved the quantity and quality of our parties until we were throwing major get-togethers. On campus, our parties became "must attend" events. Our work further solidified our TallaDallas family, and everyone around us knew ours would be a life-long friendship and love for one another that could never be broken.

As a sophomore, I decided to join a fraternity. I wanted to join in the spring of 1995, but after thinking it over, I decided against it. That summer I regretted my decision and decided that I would try again the following year. In the spring of 1996, I embarked on a long, treacherous journey with nine other young men. Due to certain circumstances, we eventually would be down to seven dedicated men. Throughout the process, we endured long days and even longer nights; but we formed a bond that I didn't think I would ever experience outside of my TallaDallas crew.

At 9:37:46 P.M., on February 28—my mother's birthday— "Sovereign 7" was initiated into the Bloody Beta Oop (Upsilon) chapter of Alpha Phi Alpha Fraternity, Inc. at Alabama State University. From my experiences in Alpha, I have seen many lines before and after me, but I swear that the genuine love the seven of us still share after 18 years is like nothing I have ever seen. We have our ups and downs, like any brothers, but we know that "my brother has always got my back." For that I am eternally grateful. Love comes in all shapes and sizes, but "true love like this is hard to find."

Extended Love

Through my natural family, my church family, my Alpha brothers, and my TallaDallas brothers, I have shown and been shown love in ways that are hard to imagine. Being part of each of these unique families has taken me far from my humble beginnings as a youth to my nurturing as a man. I can only thank God for allowing me to experience such love and support in my life. From my days on ASU's campus to my work experiences, personally or professionally, I've been able to count on my families.

For example, my family raised me to be the best man I could be. My church family brought me up with the right morals that would carry me throughout life. When I decided to pledge Alpha, I knew my TallaDallas brothers supported my decision. When I took a job in Texas, I knew Marc had my back with a place to stay and whatever else I might need. If I needed financial help, I knew TallaDallas, along with my frat brothers, were there if they could help. They all supported me in my decision to start my own mentoring business and helped me in any way they could.

As friends, the TallaDallas group has been through it all— graduations, marriages, divorces, childbirths, and even God-changing experiences. Through it all, the love we have for one another has only grown, and we've learned so much from one another. I know I speak for us all when I say we'd never change how we met, what we have been through together, and the strong bond we have formed.

People use the word *love* so casually, whether in relationships or in everyday situations; but love is genuine and should never be taken for granted. As the saying goes, "Love is what love does." As the late, great Christopher Wallace once told us, we should "spread love the Brooklyn Way," or for me, the TallaDallas way!

CHAPTER SEVEN

LIVING LIFE WITHOUT FEAR
TERRANCE TURNER

Introduction

Living life without fear? Actually, my life has always
been the opposite. I've always had fear, and I still deal with
it today because I'm far from perfect. For example, I need to
process information longer than others, I read too slowly, and
public speaking terrifies me because of my poor vocabulary
and lack of articulation.

These perceived "shortcomings" create anxiety and a lack
of confidence which leads to fear of judgment, ridicule and
failure. It didn't help that I always seemed to be a day late
and a dollar short. If I had a dollar for every time I've heard
someone say, "You almost made it," I'd be a rich man. Yet
somehow I've excelled and thrived. If I can control my fear
and make it, anyone can. Here's my story.

Childhood

I grew up in Talladega, Alabama. Even though Talladega is a
small town, it was an interesting place to live. I grew up around guys
with a lot of confidence and who knew how to sweet talk the girls.
Some of them were good athletes, and they were the type of guys
you wanted to emulate. Perhaps if they had grown up in a larger city,
more of these guys could have done great things—but I digress.

My neighborhood had kids of all ages. Demetrice Jones was my next-door neighbor. We grew up fast, and for us, it was all about trying to be cool. We were outside all day playing ball, riding bikes, picking various wild fruits, fighting dogs, and riding go-karts and mopeds. In addition to all of that, we gambled on everything, but that's just how we came up.

My father and his younger brother were the youngest of eight. They grew up in this same neighborhood, and many of their childhood friends still lived in the neighborhood. I didn't realize it at the time, but I witnessed them and the other men in my neighbor mature into responsible men; but in their younger years, they did what a lot of young men do. As such, the kids in my neighborhood were exposed to a lot: drug and alcohol use, drug dealing, gambling, and buying and selling stolen merchandise among other things.

In my neighborhood, fights were commonplace because there was always somebody beefing with somebody, but it was never anything major. However, our real interest was in girls—how to get them and what to do once you got them. Even young in the game, this was the measuring stick, but that's another book.

Although my mother and father did fairly well later in life, the early years were pretty tough. My parents; my older sister, Chonda; my younger brother, Eric; and I lived in a modest, two-bedroom house. My father also had two other children, John (Anthony) and Stephanie. They lived with their mother, but I always considered them my full brother and sister.

Things were so tight that we relied on government assistance for a while. My mother didn't get the concept of being in style. For her, it was more about making ends meet and being cost-effective. As an adult, I understand what she was doing, but as a kid it was tough to live like that. Believe me, the kids in the neighborhood let you know about it, too!

Eventually, things got better. My mother always had a job and steadily progressed in her career. My father was a brick mason and grew his business into a successful one. We then moved to a new house just yards away from our old one.

Before long, my parents started investing in real estate, which was a risk, but it paid off. They bought and sold a couple of houses and then began renovating houses to rent out. I didn't know many other people who were investing their money this way, and I was proud that my parents had the discipline and foresight to make this move. They taught me that you have to take risks in order move forward in life, and their example has served me well.

You can't be afraid to fail. The biggest mistake is never trying and playing it safe and then always regretting that you didn't go for it. You will always wonder what could have been. There is no shame in failure. Some of the most successful people in the world have failed. The biggest failure is not trying.

Additionally, from my father, I learned a strong work ethic. Ever since I could remember, my Dad was always working long hours. Many times he would work at night and on weekends to get the job done. Not only did he teach me to work hard, but he also taught me the importance of doing a job right. He always hated seeing people not taking pride in their work.

My mother was a hard worker, too. She worked a full-time job while cooking, cleaning, and ensuring that we did well in school and attended church. My mother never made excuses. She was legally blind but still excelled in juggling being a wife, a mother, and an employee. So, from my mother, I learned perseverance.

At the age of 8, she had to leave her parents, brothers and sisters, and her home in Tuscaloosa, Alabama, to come to Talladega to attend the school for the blind. Even though it was rough, she made it through her primary education and furthered her education. She then had a good career and raised a family. Whatever it took to do what needed to be done, my mother would do it.

Due to these situations, I had to grow up fast. For a long while, my Dad worked in Atlanta. My mother couldn't drive due to her disability, so I had to start driving at 12 or 13 years old. I know it seems farfetched but we had things to do and places to go, so I had to start early.

Like most kids in the South, I grew up in the church. We attended three services every Sunday—Sunday school, main service, and night service. As much as we were at church, it was inevitable that this would be the place where I met some of my best friends. In fact, these friends—Terrence ("T Hall")Hall, Anthony (Tony) Lewis, and Greg Wallace—are all members of TDI today.

We attended Ebenezer Missionary Baptist Church, and it shaped our lives dramatically. As kids, of course, going to church was not our favorite event, but we figured out how to make it fun. Girls were there, so that always made it interesting. Additionally, the other TDI guys and I learned a lot about being young men through the Crusaders (a group for young boys) and the great men that mentored us. Our pastor, Rev. B. E. McKinney made sure that he focused on the youth in our church, and his focus helped us reach our full potential.

Church is the first place where I struggled with anxiety. Anytime I had a speaking part in public (Easter program, church announcements, any speaking part), I was stressed about it leading up to the time of the event. Once I was out front to speak, my anxiety would kick into overdrive. My palms would sweat profusely, my voice would shake, and I could never find the right words.

Part of my problem was my low level of confidence. I was never a good reader, so anytime I had to read aloud, it all went wrong. My diction and pronunciation were poor. Just being from Alabama meant I was gonna have a thick Southern accent, but I think my speech was even worse than everyone else's.

Then I was self-conscious about my cheap clothes, nappy hair, and skinny body. All of this contributed to my lack of confidence and paranoia. Every time, I saw someone whispering. I was sure they were talking about me; and not having much confidence meant a rough time with social situations and dealing with girls.

Playing Ball

As a younger kid, I was tall and skinny, and I played basketball all day, every day. Even when it was 99 degrees with no shade, I was looking for a game. We had some pretty good ballers in the neighborhood. I started playing rec league, and over time I improved my game. I was tall for my age and used that to my advantage. I became the best player in my age group and I was the leader of my team. I had a great deal of confidence at that time because I had proven that I could deliver. My team was always one of the top two teams in the league and I lead us to victory many times.

Eventually, I was the only eighth grader to make the ninth grade team. Once I hit ninth grade, the other kids kept growing and I didn't. I was used to being the big man, and that had come to an end. Damn, the one thing that I was good at was no longer working for me. My confidence was gone again.

My anxiety was still with me and made me afraid anytime I had an open layup. My fear also made me overthink everything. I thought way too much, and when I did, I always conjured up the worst-case scenario in any situation. My fear of failure affected my performance, and I struggled to help the team. You can't be afraid of failure when playing sports.

Eventually, I had to give up playing organized ball all together. I never made varsity, which I always regretted. The thing was that I loved playing basketball, but my anxiety about messing up kept me from succeeding.

High School

Once I got to high school, I became a bit more comfortable with myself. I always did fairly well in school, and I eventually realized that it was an asset. I was in honors classes, and I was proud to be one of only a handful of other black students who were doing well academically. Although playing basketball was over, my new focus was to do as well as I could so one day I could make good money.

Girls were a constant focus. My game needed some work. I always ended up in the "friend zone." I just couldn't take the next step. Although I had major crushes on a few pretty girls, I never got anything to work out. I had had a few girlfriends over the years, and some treated me badly. When I got to high school, I got smarter about it. I found out that as the girls matured, they started to appreciate the smarter guys, especially if the guys weren't complete nerds.

But it wasn't the girls' fault that I didn't succeed in dating back then. It was mine. I lacked confidence and feared rejection, which was a guaranteed loss before I even started playing the game. It wasn't until I got older that I discovered that everyone gets rejected at some point. The key, however, is to stay in the game and have a short memory. Even the ones who rejected me in the past should still stay in play. Talking to girls was a confidence game, and I didn't have it. I wish I had known then what I know now.

What did boost my confidence was being one of the top students in my class. I had a good GPA, even though I was a slow reader and a poor speller. I graduated in the top ten in my class with a 3.8 GPA. However, one of my biggest mistakes was not being proactive enough in applying for scholarships. I was waiting to get my ACT test scores up and was focused on a scholarship at Tuskegee. Terrence Hall (T Hall) was trying to get a scholarship there, too.

I ended up without a significant scholarship. T Hall got a scholarship to Alabama State University, and I received a small scholarship from the Talladega Alumni Chapter, so I decided to go to ASU, too. Making that decision changed the rest of my life.

College: No Scholarship, Honors Program, and Highest Average

When I arrived in Montgomery, Alabama, I felt that this was my chance to reinvent myself. This time I would be confident and be "that guy." All of the things I was self-conscious about would be in my past. Also, I didn't want to be the nice guy anymore who lived in the friend zone. I was tired of losing and wanted to win. It was time for me to get mine.

I walked onto the campus of Alabama State with no scholarship and a chip on my shoulder. I felt slighted because there were people with full-ride scholarships but who had the same high school GPA and ACT scores as I did. The scholarship students were all given the option to be in an honors program that provided a more rigorous academic program. I was determined to figure out a way to get a scholarship, and I wanted to prove to myself that I was just as smart as anyone else on campus.

As I started my attempt to get in the honors program and receive scholarship money, I met Lorenzo Patrick, and he agreed to help me. He introduced me to the person in charge of the honors program, and I would have to convince that person to accept me into the program. After being persistent,

I was allowed into the program, but I hit a snag. All of the honors classes were full, and I was already signed up for regular classes. The only way I could finish the process of entering the honors program would be to convince the professors to add me to their already-full classes.

Being unfamiliar with the ASU campus, I didn't know my way around, and my regular classes were starting. For days, I ran around like a chicken with its head cut off trying to locate professors so I could tell them my situation. It took a lot of effort, and it seemed to take forever, but I finally got it done.

My next task was to prove that I belonged in the program. The students who took honors classes were smart and were hard-workers. Ramone Harper and T Hall were scholarship students, so they were in the program. Except for maybe one student, all the others showed exactly why they had received scholarships. With the help of my friends, I buckled down and achieved a 4.0 during my first two semesters. Sadly, though, it was only for pride because at that time, there were no scholarships available for existing students who did well after arriving at ASU.

My Major

Originally, I wanted to be a lawyer, but fear led me in a different direction. Although I've made peace with the path I chose, who knows what could have been?

I thought being a lawyer would bring money, prestige, and women. What's not to like about that? I also thought that by the time I became a lawyer, my fear of public speaking would be long gone. That didn't happen. I realized that being a lawyer but being afraid to talk in front of other people did not mix, so I would have to come up with another plan.

Given my parents' background in real estate, I thought perhaps I could be a real estate or corporate lawyer, which might not require me to do much public speaking. After asking around, I was told that majoring in accounting would be ideal for a corporate lawyer.

One of my biggest fears was that I could do all of this planning, studying, and working, only to have it all amount to nothing. Well, maybe not exactly nothing; but I kept asking myself, *If I go through all of this, work hard, and worry myself to death about tests and grades, will I end up with a decent job? Will all of this hard work pay off and land me a better job and better pay than if I had simply done the minimum to get by.*

My anxiety and uncertainty were creeping in again. I knew how my "day late and a dollar short" luck usually worked out. Could I turn that around?

I know my thinking was self-defeating. I should have been more confident and believed that my efforts would be rewarded, but I was afraid of what might not happen. Besides, the odds seemed to be stacked against me. I was feeling the pressure to deliver.

No one else in my immediate family had a four-year degree (my sister was working on it), so the expectations were great. Once I graduated, my family and friends would expect me to get a good job and make a lot of money. I also kept thinking about how much my parents had sacrificed and spent money they didn't really have so I could have a better life. I couldn't screw it up.

FBI

About halfway through college, I attended a job fair. The FBI had a recruiter there, and I talked to her about working for the agency. After our discussion, I had a good feeling about my chances. There was an internship in Washington, DC, and with my grades, the recruiter thought I was a shoe-in. I filled out the application and kept in touch with the recruiter. Soon, she told me that I had been accepted. Wow, was I excited!

I had never even been on a plane, and the furthest place I had traveled from Alabama was probably to Orlando, Florida. So, this was a big deal. I told my parents that I was going to be working with the FBI during the summer. They were proud and excited, and they told everyone.

The recruiter told me I had a few details to take care of before I could start my internship. Just protocol, she said. I had to get security clearance, and I would be asked general questions about whether I had any undisclosed items, if I had ill intent to the US government, or if I had any drug use within the last two years.

Drug use? I was never a big drug user, but I had tried smoking weed twice while hanging out at a couple of parties. What the hell? I had no idea I would be asked that. Besides, my brief dalliance with drugs had happened a year and a half ago, and I hadn't done it since.

Should I 'fess up and tell the truth, or should I take my chances with the lie detector test? Maybe if I confessed to what happened, they would understand and let me though. I was even less sure about how well I would do up against the lie detector, but I had to make it to DC. This was huge for me as well as for my family, and my parents had proudly told everyone we knew, so I couldn't let them down.

I agonized over my dilemma for weeks. I couldn't believe that this was happening. On the day of the test I still didn't know what I was going to do. I finally decided to tell the agent the truth and hope for the best. It didn't work in my favor. Although the agent was sympathetic, the rule was clear.

I couldn't face my parents with the truth. I told them that I couldn't accept the internship because I had to take a summer class that wouldn't be offered again for several semesters and missing the class would keep me from graduating. None of that was true, but I had to come up with something. When they read this book, they'll know the truth, so I should probably tell them before it comes out.

Looking back, I know now that I should have been man enough to tell my family the truth about not getting the internship back then, but this was a different type of fear. I didn't want to disappoint my parents, and I didn't want to struggle through trying to get them to understand. In retrospect, my parents would have understood even through their disappointment. The love of good parents is unconditional, and they will support you even after you mess up.

Graduation Test

Despite my failure to secure the FBI internship, things at school were going fairly well. I had a high GPA and was one of the top students in my major. The only thing I had to do was complete a standard writing test before graduating. Layup right? Besides, I was an honor student, and writing an essay would be no problem.

No so fast. The kicker was that the essay had to be on one of four topics that related to my major. Still, this shouldn't be a problem, right? Wrong. Three of the four topics were in relation to cost accounting. Cost accounting was the subject in my major that I knew the least about. My cost accounting professor didn't speak English very well, and most of the students in class could not understand him. Fortunately, I still got an A in the class since he was grading on a curve, but I didn't learn anything in his class.

I tried to brush up on cost accounting on my own, but it wasn't sinking in, so I had to rethink my strategy. I assumed the persons grading my essay were more interested in whether I could write an essay, so perhaps that would be my saving grace. I tried that and failed the test.

I was down to my last chance to pass the test and graduate on time. I talked to a few of my classmates, and everyone said, "Hey, man, don't stress it. A lot of students just write their essay ahead of time and take that into the test." I was feeling the pressure again. My family was counting on me to graduate, and I couldn't disappoint them.

I looked back over my college career, and I believed that I had done everything right; but now I needed whatever edge I could get to pass this test, so I decided to cheat. I wrote a couple of essays using reference books. People who had done this before coached me on how to shrink the essays down to almost the size of a hand.

I told myself that this was it. It was the only way. Besides, I reasoned, it wasn't my fault. Writing an essay was nothing, and I was a top accounting student; but I was forced into this unfortunate position because of a professor I couldn't understand, right? That was how I rationalized it, anyway.

Test day arrived, and I was nervous. I reminded myself that my plan could go terribly wrong. I saw two other guys I knew. They were accounting students, too, and were in the same predicament as I was. They asked if they could have a couple of my essays. They explained that since different people would be reading our essays, no one would make the connection. I was skeptical, but I thought they were good guys. I had taken most of my classes with them, and I knew they were in the same situation as I was.

After thinking it over, I gave them some of my copies, but I made it clear that if they got caught they were not to mention me. I also warned them to be careful.

I walked into the classroom, and I immediately relax a little. The class monitor was an AKPsi alumni. We knew each other, so I thought everything would work out just fine. Wrong.

My name wasn't on the list of students to take the test. What? I knew I had signed up for the test. I was sent to the testing office where I discovered that other students were having the same problem. The good news was that they would allow us to take the test. The bad news was that it would be in another classroom, and the monitor looked like a stickler—in other words, no cheating. The first thing she said to us when we entered the classroom was, "No games! Anything suspicious, and I won't accept your test!" Damn, I can't win, but what choice did I have?

I looked at the three options of essays that I could write, and it didn't take long to see that they all related to cost accounting. After the test got underway, I tried to pull out my essay. I started to write, but I was having trouble because I was seated right in front of the class monitor. Since I arrived late to the test location, all of the premium seats in the back were already taken. So I was front and center, and the monitor was being especially vigilant.

I pulled out my essay and started writing. At that moment, the monitor looked up. Nervous, I flinched, and the essay fell to the floor. Great move! This was like being on the free throw line in the NBA finals—two shots to win the game—and the first free throw is an air ball. Damn, dude!

I was frozen with fear. What should I do? If I bend down to get the essay, the monitor might see me. Then I'm done. If I wait until she walks around the classroom, she might look down and see it. So with my foot, I tried to slide the essay toward me, but I couldn't get it. Then I saw the monitor move. She was getting up! Change of plan. I decided to erase everything I had written so no one could tie the exposed essay to me.

When the monitor saw the essay, she asked, "Whose is this?" She directed the question to everyone in my general area. Everyone denied culpability. She questioned us again and said that someone needed to own up to it. I wasn't going to confess. You would have to have me on tape on that one. The monitor kept the essay and went back to her desk.

I dodged a big one, but I still had a problem. I didn't have an essay. So I decide to write an essay about the one accounting topic that didn't relate to cost accounting. I just had to "shoot the three" and see what happened.

I left the classroom hoping the grader would accept my essay based on how well it was written. I reasoned that it was actually a writing test, not an accounting test.

I couldn't have been more wrong. I failed the test. Damn! I knew I couldn't graduate without passing the test, so how was I going to figure this out? I went to the chair of the accounting department, Dr. Crawford. I told her that the reason I performed so poorly on the test was because I wrote on the subject I knew most about, which wasn't cost accounting.

Dr. Crawford was not only the chair of the department, but she was my first accounting teacher. She appreciated that I was smart and that I cared about doing well. She always wanted to see young black men succeed, and she tried her best to help us. When I told her my version of what happened, she just shook her head. "Mr. Turner," she said, "you must do better."

Dr. Crawford told me that she would see what she could do, but she couldn't make any promises. In the meantime, graduation was fast approaching, and my parents and family were making preparations for the big celebration. I was nervous as hell. I couldn't concentrate on finishing up my classes because I was stressing about graduating. As a result, I ended up making my only C in college in an auditing class. I'm still mad about that.

Finally, I heard from Dr. Crawford. Together, she and I went to plead my case with Dean Vaughn. He drilled me about what happened, but he agreed to help. Eventually, he was able to secure for me another opportunity to take the test.

Though I had another chance, I still had a problem with cost accounting. This time, I would be smarter. I wrote all three essays and then memorized them word for word. This took some doing, but I was determined to pass the test. After taking the test, I felt pretty good, but graduation was approaching, and I needed more than just a good feeling before I could feel completely confident.

It came down to the eleventh hour. I couldn't even enjoy my last days before graduation. Although I went to the parties and hung out, I couldn't feel comfortable because I didn't know if I would walk.

Finally, I got confirmation that I had passed the test and would graduate. Sadly, the graders matched an essay to one of the guys I had given an essay. He wasn't able to graduate, and I felt badly about that; but dude never gave me up—standup guy. But, here's the deal. All the excuses that I gave above about why I needed to cheat on the test was some bull. There was no good reason; I was just afraid to fail. Afraid to figure out cost accounting on my own, failing the test and not graduating. But I could have figured it out. I eventually figured out how to pass the test without cheating. The whole episode was just stupid. Take it from me, don't let fear of failure push you towards the perceived easy route. This could have turned out very badly for me. Could have destroyed something that took a lifetime to build... my reputation.

I finished college with a great GPA but no job. I knew that I wanted to work for a CPA firm, but I didn't have enough hours to sit for the CPA exam, so I decided to go to graduate school. I ended up getting an assistantship to go to the University of Arkansas. One of my professors at Alabama State was there working on his doctorate, and he told me that money was available for minorities (good looking out).

After graduate school, I landed a job at one of the largest accounting firms in the world at the time, Arthur Anderson in Dallas, Texas. I passed the CPA exam and became a certified public accountant. I did well at Anderson as an auditor and progressed within the organization. I eventually transferred to the Atlanta office and took a positions working in Anderson's Merger and Acquisitions group.

After Anderson, I moved to my current employer where I've served as director of finance, director of operations, and director of strategic planning. Currently, I serve as the vice president of finance for my division where I oversee all aspects of finance and accounting.

In my various roles, I've been involved in business start-ups, major investment evaluations, acquisition integrations, product moves, compensation plan development, and various strategic initiatives. I've traveled to various regions of the world and interacted with people of various cultures. I make good money. I'm married to a beautiful wife, have two great kids, and live in a great neighborhood.

My point in laying out my successes is to make the point that if I can achieve, anyone can who has the determination and the drive. Even though I've struggled with anxiety and fear, I've been able to work through my fears and not let them keep me from being successful. Even though public speaking is still not my strongest skill, I'm at least comfortable enough to do it when I need to. I relied on my other assets to further my career. First, no one will ever out work me. I'll do whatever it takes to get the job done... if that means no sleep than so be it. Secondly, I've always developed positive win/win relationships. Not only with my TDI brothers, but with others in my professional life. These people have helped me tremendously and I've always tried to help them as much as possible. Lastly, I've always maintained a positive attitude towards other people. These attributes have served me well. It goes without saying that my TDI team helped me overcome y fears also. Everyone has fears or things they're self-conscience about. So "Living Life Without Fear" probably won't be your claim to fame, either. The key is to attack life anyway, and if you fail, get back up and try again until you succeed. If I can do it, anyone can!

CHAPTER EIGHT

STEREOTYPES OF A BLACK MALE MISUNDERSTOOD, AND IT'S STILL ALL GOOD

ANTHONY LEWIS, Ph.D

Research states that a single-parent family background and the poverty that usually accompanies it render children twice as likely to drop out of high school, 2.5 times as likely to become out-of-wedlock teen parents, and 1.4 times as likely to be unemployed. These children miss more days of school, have lower educational aspirations, receive lower grades, and eventually divorce more often as adults. They are almost twice as likely to exhibit antisocial behavior as adults; 25 to 50 percent more likely to manifest such behavioral problems as anxiety, depression, hyperactivity, or dependence; two to three times more likely to need psychiatric care; and much more likely to commit suicide as teenagers.

Based on those numbers and percentages alone, I was doomed at birth. I didn't stand a chance. December 12, 1975, around 1:30 A.M., Diann Lewis, an unmarried black mother, went into labor at Citizens Hospital in Talladega, Alabama, preparing to give birth to her second child.

She took me home—well, not our home, but the place she called home—to live with her mother and father, my grandparents,

Cecil and Vicie "MuDear" Lewis. Dad was simply not there, and I would not see him as far as I can recall until I was a toddler. I do remember one instance where he would come to my grandparents' house to bring me a bag of candy, but I wouldn't take it. The audacity, to leave my mother to raise me and not give her financial support, and he thought the gift of candy would work? Momma wasn't raising a fool—she got this! The void that was there was filled by the prayers and care of two of the most caring grandparents, MuDear and Granddaddy.

The Early Years

We continued living with my grandparents until I was three years old. Then my mother and my older brother, Donnell, would move into my Uncle Willie Joe Lewis's two-bedroom trailer across from Knoxville Homes Housing Projects.

These were the times I remember the most. My mother would share her love of music with me. We didn't have air conditioning, so on a steamy summer evening, we would spend countless nights with the trailer door open, listening to her favorite 45's and albums. At times, when we were not listening to music, we would just sit and listen to the sounds of the night and watch the lightening bugs fly by. To me, life was good.

My mother was a kindergarten teacher but changed careers and became a bookkeeper. She would later go back to her first love, working with children in the field of education. I didn't realize it at the time, but the seed of working with disadvantaged children was being planted in me.

If we were poor, I did not know it. Everything seemed fine because every Sunday morning, Sunday afternoon, and Wednesday evening, my mother took Donnell and me to Greater Ebenezer Missionary Baptist Church. There, our pastor, the late Rev. B. E. McKinney, would tell us we were blessed. I did not know what that meant, but when people would say it, they always had a smile on their faces, so I thought everything was fine.

Six years later, we would move to a place we could call our own. My mother is a bargain shopper, and most of what she bought for us was on sale, on clearance, or from a yard sale; but we were content. And yes, we were always sharp! She would dress us so nicely that Uncle Will would always remind us that there was no reason for us to misbehave, given how much our mother did for us. In 1985, Momma would take her bargaining skills to the bank, where she managed to buy a repossessed trailer for us to live in.

That two-bedroom, single-wide trailer was probably a 1978 model, but it was still nice. It even had black and white shag carpet. This was not just a trailer; this was our home.

The Elementary Years

I attended Central Elementary School as an A Honor Roll student from first grade through fourth grade. All of my teachers at Central—Mrs. Sims, Mrs. Lawrence, Mrs. Willis, and Mrs. Thompson— all would say I was a smart little boy. They would also say I was quiet and shy. I didn't talk much unless I absolutely had to. Sometimes I was teased because I had a stuttering problem and would spend some of my class time and some summers with Ms. Hill, my speech teacher.

I can remember going on the playground and listening to my friends brag to one another about the jobs their fathers had and defensively arguing, "My daddy can beat your daddy up." This was a conversation and argument that I would sit on the sidelines to watch. I could not participate because I did not know what type of job my daddy had, let alone his fighting capabilities.

While at Central, I had my first fight with a white boy who pushed me down the slide. I was in front of him, and he was waiting to slide down. He was rushing me and eventually pushed me down the slide. I waited for him at the bottom of the slide and then punched him, leaving him with a bloody nose. I was suspended, but he wasn't. Still, I had my mother's support. She came to my school to advocate for her baby. Her concern was that I was suspended and the white boy was not.

The summer before my fourth grade year, I experienced my first challenge. I wanted Mrs. Moreland as my fourth grade teacher. Donnell and my cousins Eric, Antoine, and Terry had her; but I was put in Mrs. Thompson's class. You see, Mrs. Thompson was known as one of the meanest, hardest teachers you would never want. She never smiled, and she walked through the halls wearing gray suits that would accent her silver hair. I thought her part-time job was that of a witch.

I cried all summer because I knew that my straight A's could possibly turn into straight F's. My mother would have one of her many talks with me about how she believed in me and that I could do anything I put my mind to. She would remind me that with God, all things are possible; but I wasn't sure God knew about Sadie Thompson's class.

I approached this with much reluctance. I knew that if I were to pass Mrs. Thompson's class, I had better stay ahead of the game. I would write my spelling words five times each before they were even due. I would answer the chapter reviews in the back of my book before they were due. I would always stay one step ahead of her. This old white lady was not going to fail me.

Through hard work, fear of that mean lady, and staying ahead of her, I made the A Honor Roll every six weeks while I was in her class. I also realized that she only wanted the best for her students. In fact, I became one of her favorite students.

Later that year, I found out that Central was going to close, and I would have to go to Houston Elementary School, a brand-new school. I would only have to attend for one year, my fifth grade year.

The Church House

My mother kept us in church every time the doors were open. Not only were we in church, we were actively involved. We were members of the Sun Beams, the Stair-Steppers Choir, and the Crusaders ("Once a Crusader, always a Crusader"). Even though I enjoyed the Sun Beams and the Stair-Steppers, which both had female advisors, there was nothing like the Crusaders.

The Crusaders was an all-male church group with male advisors. Perhaps I was drawn to the group because of the missing father in my life. Even though my granddaddy was a father figure I would see regularly, I was still missing my real father figure.

The Crusaders' advisors—my Uncle Karl, Leon, Billy Joe (Co-Pilot), and George—were there every Sunday to teach us not only about the Bible and serving others, but to act as the father figure I was missing. They spent time with us and took us on trips to Six Flags and many other places. We considered our church, The Greater Ebenezer Missionary Baptist Church, to have the best Crusaders chapter in the State of Alabama. We were competitive. We raised the most money, and we had the best Crusader choir.

Not only did we have lots of fun, but our advisors were not afraid to correct us when we were wrong. I had much respect for them, and I liked being around them. I wanted to be like them, much like a son looks at his father.

Middle School Years

I joined the beginner's band in sixth grade at Dixon Middle School and continued through eighth grade at Zora Ellis Junior High School. I knew then I wanted to play my trumpet as a member of the Tiger Marching Band at Talladega High School. But would I make it?

I made some bad decisions and misbehaved in school. I also began to pay less attention to English, math, and science and paid more attention to Renee, Dee-Dee, and Lorene. My Aunt Fannie said I was "smelling myself."

I got my first paddling from the principal because I cursed at a teacher. We were lining up to go to lunch when Ms. Cook told the class to be quiet. I continued to talk, and she put my name on the board. To show out for the girls, I continued to talk, and she put a check by my name. As we walked out of the classroom, I said, "All I know is you better erase that damn check by my name." Little did I know, the librarian, Mrs. Adams, was across the hall and heard what I said. She took me to the office.

After the paddling at school, I got a whipping at home. Were these behaviors typical of a child from a single-parent home? Was this the beginning of behaviors that would lead to a dropout?

The College Itch

My mother would begin taking us to the Magic City Classic and the Turkey Day Classic when we were just kids. The Magic City Classic is a football rivalry game held in Birmingham, Alabama, between Alabama State University and Alabama A&M University. The Turkey Day Classic in Montgomery is the oldest black college classic. It pits Alabama State University against Tuskegee University.

It was at the Turkey Day Classic that I fell in love with the Alabama State University Mighty Marching Hornets. I knew I wanted to be part of that band. Maybe it was their marching style, which I was not accustomed to but tried to duplicate in the Talladega Band. Maybe it was the feathered plumes blowing in the wind. Whatever it was, I knew that one day I would be a Marching Hornet!

During my senior year in high school, with my cousins Terry and Michael and my friend Terrance all off at college at

ASU, I made frequent trips to Montgomery to see them on the campus of Alabama State University. On one particular visit, during an R. Kelly concert at what was then the Joe L. Reed Acadome, there was a party at Michael's house on Westhaven Avenue, not far from campus. I started life-long friendships with several of the guys there. This is when I was introduced to the boys from Dallas, Texas.

My education was more important than an overnight trip.

I would have been considered a fool had I dropped out of high school. According to statistics, a black male raised by a single mother— stereotyped yet misunderstood—I would have never made it, but I did. I graduated from Talladega High School in May 1994.

I'm a College Student

When I arrived on the campus of Alabama State University in the summer of 1994 for band pre-drill, I began my journey of becoming a Mighty Marching Hornet. Getting up at 4:00 A.M. every morning as a "crab" to run, work out, march, and run again was painful. We would march everywhere, even to the cafeteria, singing, "So-o-o-o hard, so hard to be a ho-o-o-ornet, so hard to be a ho-o-o-o-rnet, so hard to be a marching hornet, na na na na na."

While not "crabbing" the band and missing classes, I was out kicking it with the boys from Dallas and my boys from Talladega. We came to be known as TallaDallas. I was a freshman, the only freshman of the crew, and they were sophomores and juniors.

Their classes were on Tuesdays and Thursdays; and mine were on Mondays, Wednesdays, and Fridays. So when the rest of the guys were out of class, it was extremely difficult for me to go to class on a sunny Montgomery Monday. While they were barbequing, I would have to go to class. While they went to the Montgomery Mall, I would have to go to class. While they were in Columbus, Georgia, I would have to go to class.

The way I figured it, I could miss one class to go kick it with the fellas. That one class would turn into two classes and then three classes. Then the A's turned into B's, then C's, and then D's. I was willing to miss class and let my grades slip just to spend time with TallaDallas—my boys, my brothers.

As I continued to miss classes and watch my grades slip, I lost my band scholarship, as well as other financial aid. However, I had to stay in school. I couldn't leave my brothers. I could not afford not to be in the presence of TallaDallas. I considered dropping out of college and going to truck driving school in Montgomery just to stay connected to TallaDallas, but my brother Donnell would later talk me out of that. Perhaps, I was convinced to stay in school when I saw him walk across the stage to receive his degrees from Troy University in Troy, Alabama. I had to stay in school, but I had no financial aid.

So I did what any man would do. I got a job! For the next couple of semesters I worked at Food World, a grocery store on Atlanta Highway, and went to school part-time. I worked about 32 hours a week at the grocery store, so how was I going to find the time to kick it with the crew? I would make it happen. I took chances.

One Friday night, the crew decided to go to Columbus, Georgia, which is about 90 miles east of Montgomery. It was kind of late, and I noticed that the fellas were packing overnight bags, just in case they decided not to come back that night. No big deal, right? Well, there was one minor issue. I had to go to work the next morning at 10:00. But I reasoned that even if they decided to stay overnight, we could get up early the next morning and head back in time for me to make it to work. I had this thing planned out—or at least I thought I did.

Ramone Harper looked at me, head to the side, and said, "Tony Lewis? Don't go!" I was shocked. I argued, "What do you mean? If we come back tonight, I can make it to work in the morning. If not, will you guys get up early in time for me to make it back to work?" Ramone looked at me again. "Tony Lewis? Don't do it!"

I thought about it. I needed my job to help pay for school, and there would be other times to go to Columbus. My education was more important than an overnight trip that could possibly get me fired if I didn't make it back on time. So I got in the car and, as my grandfather would say, down the road we had business. Interstate 85, Columbus, Georgia, here we come!

We had a great time in Columbus! We had so much fun that we could not make it back the same night, so we had to get a hotel and spend the night. I reminded the fellas that I needed to be at work the next morning at 10:00 and asked who was going to take me back. Ramone and Marc joined in unison and said, "Tony Lewis, we told you not to come." The next morning, I would have to call in with the raspy voice to tell my boss that I was sick. Luckily, it worked.

The Bond Was Purposeful

There were many similar episodes and illogical decisions that we all made. To this day, I wonder how we are still alive or how we are not in jail. The hand of God was all over our lives for He had a purpose for us.

The TallaDallas bond was strengthened by our constant togetherness. We did everything together. The parties we threw, the trips we took, the events we attended—all made our bond that much stronger.

Did I mention the parties we hosted? I began my love for being a DJ from the early TallaDallas parties. Because of the TallaDallas parties, I am also the owner of SugaBear Entertainment (SBE)—DJ and Sound Services.

There was one party in particular we called the "No More Than 1,000 Party." This meant that we were not going to let the 1,001st person in. We were charging $10. People were coming in. We went up to $20, and they still were coming in. Once we reached 1,000 patrons, we did not let anyone else in. Now, I was a special education major, not a math major, but at minimum we profited $10,000. Come on, Granddaddy! Down the road we had business. I-85, Columbus, Georgia, here we come!

The purpose of our bond was to encourage one another, from encouraging me not to go to Columbus to encouraging one another never to give up, encouraging one another to do it and do it big. This encouragement helped me finally to pass college algebra after three tries. This encouragement and bond helped me to endure and become a member of Kappa Alpha Psi Fraternity, Incorporated. This encouragement helped me finally to finish my four-year degree in only eight years, but I didn't stop there.

After receiving a bachelor's degree in special education, I received my master's degree two years later. I didn't stop there. I received another master's degree in educational administration. I didn't stop there. This misunderstood black male from a single-parent home received his Ph.D. in educational leadership and policy analysis from the University of Missouri. Yeah, and it's still all good!

The Fruits of the Bond

I began my work career as a special education teacher at Jefferson Davis High School in Montgomery, Alabama, where I taught for six years. While there, I was advisor to the Junior Civitans International, winning them numerous awards and recognitions.

Next, I was appointed to assistant principal and then principal of E. D. Nixon Elementary School, a position I held for five years. While at E. D. Nixon, I oversaw many achievements, including the charter of the school's first National Elementary School Honor Society, televisions mounted in all classrooms, six 52 inch flat-screens placed throughout the school, laptops and projectors given to all teachers, discipline decreased by more than 50 percent, daily student attendance increased, and most importantly the school became an Alabama Torchbearer

School during the 2007-2008 school year (one of only nine in the state) and again during the 2010-2011 school year (one of only eleven in the state).

Being an Alabama Torchbearer School is a prestigious award given by the State of Alabama recognizing high-poverty schools (97 percent poverty rate at Nixon) where 90 percent or more of the students exceed national averages on Stanford Achievement Tests (SAT-10) and the Alabama Reading and Mathematics Test (ARMT). Because of this award and making Adequate Yearly Progress (AYP), the school was awarded more than $75,000. The school was also ranked number 18 out of 706 schools in the state.

In May 2011, I was nominated to be the only principal in the State of Alabama published in the inaugural edition of *Who's Who in Black Alabama*. Because of my successes in Alabama, I was heavily recruited to work in the Kansas City (Missouri) School District, one of the lowest performing districts in the nation. Currently, I am the Director of Elementary Schools in the Department of School Leadership for Kansas City Public Schools, where I oversee 26 schools. And it's still all good!

CHAPTER NINE

AND MY WHOLE CREW IS LOUNGIN', CELEBRATIN' EVERY DAY, NO MORE PUBLIC HOUSIN'
HERMAN MONCRIEF

As I sit and gather my thoughts to document my brief life up to this moment, there's one word that resonates with me being in the place that I am in today: *choice*. A *choice* is an act of selecting or making a decision when faced with two or more possibilities. Having the ability to make a decision, good or bad, is paramount to being alive.

In my opinion, there is nothing more defeating than not having the ability to choose. Whether you are choosing between good or bad, right or wrong, left or right, you have the ability to choose, and that ability to make a choice is powerful.

It's no coincidence that the adjectives of the word *choice* are ones that indicate the best (*excellent, exclusive, prime, exquisite, precious, rare*). So the word *choice* is sacred to me, and I continue to put myself in situations that afford me the ability to choose. If you are going to choose, choose to be great, choose to make an impact, choose to become a leader of men, and above all else choose situations that continually allow you to have a CHOICE.

Happy Hollow

I was born on Saturday, September 9, 1972, at the Professional Center Hospital in Montgomery, Alabama. My parents, along with their parents, were from nearby Prattville, a city approximately 11 miles northwest of where I took my first breath. I spent my early youth in the section of Prattville affectionately known as Happy Hollow, or The Hollow to its residents.

The Hollow was recognized with a historical marker on August 2, 2010. A passage from that marker reads: "A traditional African American neighborhood, the Hollow was home for domestic workers, farm laborers, landowners, and sharecroppers. Descendants of these families became leaders in Prattville and beyond: educators, nurses, doctors, accountants, carpenters, armed forces, and ministers." So there was something special about The Hollow and the people who called it home.

I spent much of my time in The Hollow playing with my cousins and visiting my grandmother's house every day, which was only a short distance through the path from my neighborhood, Smith Quarters. My childhood there was one of joy, as my foundation was secured, and I always reflect fondly on growing up in The Hollow. We lived on Harlem Street in a neighborhood of Jim Walter homes known as Smith Quarters. Residents of The Hollow named the neighborhood Smith Quarters after the white owner of all the homes on our street.

I remember how the walls in our house would sweat during the winters. I could never quite understand why and how this occurred, and since all of my neighbors' homes did the same thing, I thought it was normal. Little did I know that the moisture was caused by a buildup of condensation due to poor insulation. We were still as happy as could be, despite the circumstances at the time.

My parents were blue-collar workers. Dad worked for several different factories, as did most of the men in my community. There wasn't a day that went by when I didn't see men in the neighborhood rise early and head out to work to provide for their families. My mom was employed at department stores during my early childhood. Still, my parents always found a way to provide for our family, even if it meant we ate and they didn't. My parents taught me to be resilient and faithful, even when things are at their worst.

The members of my family have always been close, and they always encouraged me to be the best I can be. I don't think there was one single day growing up when I didn't visit my grandmothers. Lizzie Mae Bowman and Beulah "London" Moncrief were two of the most amazing people I ever met. To this day, I can still pull from the archives of wisdom I received from each of those women and apply it to my current life. Both of them were amazingly strong and had an abundance of love for their families.

Lizzie taught me the value of a dollar and how to make a dime work like a dollar. She never had a lot of anything but seemed to always have everything she needed. It was amazing to see her provide for so many and ask for nothing in return.

London, as everyone affectionately called her, instilled in me confidence and made sure I knew who I was and how special I was because of the name I carried. I can vividly remember her telling me I am a Moncrief, and that that means something. I've never known Grandma to mince words. If she had something to say, she would say it no matter who liked it or not. I always admired her candidness.

Both of my grandmothers had a major impact on my life. They had a close relationship with Christ, gave unconditionally, and loved me no matter what the situation. Coincidently, Lizzie and London passed away two weeks a part in 2005, just months after my twins were born.

Teenage Years

Being from a small town, sports were a major part of my life. From the time I was six or seven years old, I was involved in some sort of organized sporting activity. Whether it was basketball, football, or baseball, my mom made it her business always to have me involved in some type of extracurricular activity.

When I was a child, our family doctor diagnosed me as hyperactive. Back then there wasn't an official clinical diagnosis for being ADD or ADHD. I don't think there was any Ritalin or Adderall, so hyperactivity was not understood as a disability. Instead, you were just labeled as being "bad as hell," which is how many identified me throughout my childhood and early teen years.

By the time I was seven or eight, my family moved into a new neighbor approximately a mile or two from The Hollow. By that time, I was already known as a badass kid by most of the people who knew me and soon would be known that way by people who didn't.

Before I continue, I need to expound on my behavior problems and how they impacted my life. I was always known to have a bad temper and a rotten attitude (hated to lose at anything), and I gravitated to mischievous activities. I was always rebellious, and to a certain extent, I still am today. I never liked authority. I always wanted to try things even when someone said I shouldn't, and I never thought about the consequences until after the fact.

My behavior made life for my parents, especially my mom, really interesting. Mom would take my siblings and me everywhere with her. If you ever saw Yvonne, she would have her four kids in tow. To the disdain of many people we came in contact with, Mom had me with her, so they knew I was apt to cause some type of trouble such as fighting with their kids, breaking something, or doing something totally disruptive. I'm sure Mom routinely had to apologize for my behavior, but the one thing she never did was tell me I would not be something.

Mom always was in my corner, no matter the situation. Even when some people saw me as nothing more than a badass kid, she saw something more. I don't think I could ever thank her enough for believing in me.

Sports was my one true outlet, it was the arena where I began to channel my anger and develop the skill necessary to put myself in a position of power, by creating situations in which I could have a choice. When my parents signed me up for football, I was this scrawny, nappy-headed, 45-pound kid with a big mouth and a bad attitude. I constantly was reprimanded and had to do extra laps, bear crawls, and sprints because of my bad attitude.

During my first years playing ball, the coaches didn't have a clue what to do with me, so I played nose guard. Yep, at 45 pounds (in full gear), I was in the middle of the line of scrimmage. I believe someone realized I was quick and too stupid to be afraid, so why not put me right over the center? I actually performed well and loved the contact, although in most cases I was in the backfield before the center could look up.

It was when I was around 12 or 13 that I finally started to grow out of some of my bad habits. Dad always told me about temperament and maintaining my cool. He would look me in the eye and say that no matter how good I am at anything, none of that will matter if I can't control my temper. Being a hothead was not a quality becoming of a leader, so he would say. At that time I wasn't even aware that being a leader was anywhere in my future, but maybe Dad was prophetic in a way, because it was around that time when I started playing quarterback in the youth league.

Playing quarterback gave me a different purpose and a feeling that was like no other I had experienced. I would compare it to being a pitcher because I felt like I could control a ballgame, but there was something different about being a quarterback. I was the leader of a group for the first time, and they responded as I responded. Knowing that people were following my lead and that my actions had an impact on people other than myself, being a quarterback empowered me. I felt obligated to be a better person, be a better teammate, be a LEADER.

By the time I got to high school, my identity was more so aligned with sports than with just being the bad kid in the neighborhood. Although I still had my challenges, I was much more reserved, and I demonstrated a level head, especially on the football field.

One day while playing in the youth league, a coach pulled me aside and told me I would be the first person of color to play quarterback at my high school. This was the mid-80's, 21 years after the passage of the Civil Rights bill. At the time, I didn't believe him primarily because there were a number of guys who had come before me who were significantly more talented than I was and never had the chance to play the position at a varsity level. Like me, they played the position in youth league and maybe junior varsity. Somehow, though, when it came to the varsity level, being the face of the most important sport in Prattville never happened to a person of color.

Dad always told me that I shouldn't change positions, no matter what. He encouraged me to have patience and to wait my turn, and that is what I did. It was not until 1989, my junior year in high school, that I got my first opportunity to take the reins. We made the playoffs that year, and during the last game of the season, the starting quarterback suffered a season-ending injury.

During the week leading up to the game, friends I'd known since kindergarten said to me, "You know you are not going to start. They are going to start the other guy." You might think those discouraging words would have bothered me or made me doubt whether I was going to get my shot; but what my friends didn't know was that first thing Monday morning of that week, I was summoned to the head coach's office. He told me I was his starter for Friday night, and he was confident that I would do a great job. He also told me not to listen to any of the noise and just to show up Friday night ready to play. I was excited and nervous, but more than anything, I was confident because I was prepared.

The morning before the game, Dad woke me up around 5:00 A.M. to chat about the game. He reminded me to handle myself accordingly, to make good decisions, and to keep a cool head. This would be the start of a Friday morning routine that lasted throughout my high school football career. However, that particular morning Dad told me if anyone asked how it felt to be the first person of color to play quarterback at my school, I should simply tell them I'm just like all the other quarterbacks, no difference at all.

What Next?

Although sports had a profound impact on my life, I would be remiss if I didn't mention that sports also had a negative impact on my life. How could something so positive morph into a negative?

In hindsight, the negative was always there, but I just never acknowledged its presence. Like we do with most things in life, we tend to magnify the things that make us feel good. So in my case, I liked how being the quarterback made me feel. I liked having teachers tell me what a great game I played or that they saw my picture in the Saturday morning paper. Because of my success as an athlete, I was given the benefit of the doubt more times than not, especially when it came to academics.

Now, let me clarify this whole "benefit of the doubt thing," because today we hear how athletes are given everything because of their success on the field, and this doesn't just apply to athletes. Special treatment is prevalent throughout society whenever people achieve a certain status or become proficient at something society deems to be significant or important.

I spent more time honing my athletic skills and directed little of my energy at developing my academic skillset. This was a huge negative byproduct of being somewhat decent in athletics. I never thought myself to be a gifted athlete; actually, it was just the opposite. I always knew there were many guys who possessed way more talent than me. My approach to sports was to work hard at my craft, and what I lacked in physical gifts and tools, I would make up with mental acumen—in a football sense, not in the world of academia.

I performed well enough academically to get by, and my effort was mediocre at best. I had little interest in being the smart guy in the room. Outside of sports, I wanted to blend in with the rest of the student body. I wanted to be accepted by peers and be a cool guy, and of course I wanted to be noticed by girls, so I prioritized all of those things ahead of studying and preparing myself for any type of collegiate endeavor that didn't involve sports.

At my school, there was a wall in the main hallway where all the "cool guys" would hang out. It was my freshman year, and I so badly wanted to be on that wall with those guys simply because all the girls liked the cool guys. I was set to take my first algebra class, but I noticed that most of the guys on that wall had this one math book with a Levi's jeans pocket on the cover. I discovered that it was a general math book for a class that was a level below Algebra I. Despite being at a higher level in math, I wanted that book and decided to drop my algebra class so I could take the general math class. That is just one example of how I prioritized academics at that time in my life.

I didn't prioritize academics at that time in my life.

All good things must come to an end, and what I believed at that time to be my good thing ended in the winter of 1989 with my last high school football game. I graduated high school in May 1990. My high school coach found an opportunity for me to continue my athletic career at a small two-year school located in Mississippi. I was happy about the opportunity and worked hard during the summer months to prepare.

Shortly after arriving in Mississippi, it did not take long for me to realize that football may not be a long-term career option for a player like me. I was there with guys who were athletically gifted and had come to that tiny school from other major universities only because they didn't qualify academically. I was there looking for an opportunity, but there wasn't any notoriety for me at all—just the word of my coach and a few of my game films.

Ultimately, I decided to leave shortly after fall camp, and it was on the bus ride back to Prattville that I was faced with the question, What next? Once I was back home, I felt totally lost in the sense that I had no clue what I wanted to do with my life. Up to that point, my life was totally centered around sports, and as far as I knew I would be playing sports for at least a few more years.

Around that same time, the conversations I had with my dad also changed. I always wanted to get a job when I was in high school, but Dad would always say don't worry about working right now because you will be working the rest of your life. However, a couple weeks after returning from my failed attempt at collegiate ball, my Dad woke me up early once again, but this time the conversation was different. He let me know that I needed to get up and find a job.

Not only was this an uncertain time for me, but it was a trying time for my parents, too. After over 20 years of marriage, they decided to divorce. The timing could not have been worse. I was already wandering around trying to figure out who I was and where I was going, and now my parents were about to go their separate ways. It was tough watching my parents go through the process—two people I loved unconditionally on opposite sides of the room discussing property and child-support payments.

Subsequent to my parents' divorce, I moved with my Mom to a new neighborhood not far from where I grew up. I got a job at a local plant and started to accept that my path had changed.

For a while life didn't seem so bad. I had a job and more money in my pocket than I'd ever had before. I was staying home with Mom so when I ate my whole family ate. I didn't have any financial responsibilities, so I helped Mom keep current on her obligations, and things were good—or so I thought.

I spent most of my days after work drinking with friends. Drinking became one of my favorite pastimes. My drinking didn't just start after high school. I had a group of good friends (including my older brother) I would hang out with, and we were known as the drinking crew. We were just a group of guys who knew how to have a good time. We worked the clubs every weekend. Actually, we would start on Thursday night and party straight through until Sunday.

My cousin Lavell Adair (RIP) was one of my closest friends. We grew up on adjacent streets, and I spent more time at his house than I did my own. He was a year younger than me and was set to come out of high school in the summer of 1991. He would always talk about attending college after high school and wanted to leave the state and attend Florida A&M University. Ultimately, he settled on attending Alabama A&M University and talked me into attending along with him.

Initially, I hesitated because I didn't believe I was adequately prepared. Since I no longer had sports as my crutch, what was I going to do in college? I didn't put much effort into academics in high school, so I didn't think I was at all prepared to attend anyone's university. However, what I didn't know was that certain historically black colleges and universities (HBCUs) would conditionally accept students, waiving the minimum GPA or standardized test score requirement.

So in the fall of 1991, along with my cousin, I enrolled at Alabama A&M University (AAMU). Upon arrival, I instantly felt as if I was part of something positive. Even then, though, I still didn't value the opportunity that was in front of me. I made friends easily in my dorm and spent a good bit of time hanging out in and around campus. From the first week, I was known by every dorm monitor (or "count," as we called them) who worked in my building. I was out every night until after midnight, mainly drinking and smoking and living it up.

The count stopped me my first week on campus and told me I needed to slow down. He told me that I had only been on campus one week, and he already knew my name because I was the last and the loudest person coming in each night. But even though I was out every night, I attended all of my classes every day. I managed to carve out decent grades, but I still didn't realize the positive impact academics could have on my life.

Just as with most college students, money was an issue. Most of the time my cousin looked out for me, giving me money or food anytime he would receive some from his mom or grandmother. I never wanted to call home and ask for money because my mom was divorced and taking care of my two younger sisters. I didn't want to ask my dad for money either because I was an adult and thought I should have been able to take care of myself.

Mom sent whatever she could. The best times were when she came up on some food stamps! It was like Christmas. I would give a guy twenty bucks in stamps to take me to the market and come back with groceries! I had a footlocker in my dorm room, and when I had stamps, it was full to the brim with vienna sausages, ramen noodles, Little Debbie snack cakes, and all kinds of goodies. I sold most of it. You don't know how valuable a can of vienna sausages or a pack of ramen noodles are until you are in college. However, those holidays were few and far in between, and most nights it was hunger pains until the Caf opened the next morning for breakfast.

There was an eatery on campus called The Greasy Spoon. One night, I was so hungry that I went to The Spoon with a couple of friends. I didn't have one cent to my name, but I got in line anyway and tried to lift a chicken sandwich. Unfortunately, the lady working the line saw me and pulled me to the side. She didn't make a scene or call the campus police. Instead, she told me that she saw what I did and that I didn't have to steal. She told me that if I was hungry and needed something that I should have just asked for it. I was so appreciative and humbled by her kindness.

That's when I realized that many of the HBCUs are an extension of our communities with people helping one another. That woman's compassion was exactly the type of caring I was accustomed to while growing up in The Hollow.

Partying all the time takes money because everything has a cost: a fee to get in the club and money for drinks and food. Even random dorm/house parties required some cash, primarily for the alcohol. I was always looking for ways to get cash for alcohol.

Once, my two roommates and I decided we didn't necessarily

need money to get beer. There was a convenience store on the corner that was full of beer, so who needs money? I came up with a plan to walk in calmly and walk out with three cases of beer—one case per person. Everyone was in except my cousin. He wanted to be part of the caper, but I wouldn't let him. My thinking at the time was that he was doing something positive with his life and didn't need to screw it up doing something stupid with me. On the other hand, I was just killing time at AAMU, so I had nothing to lose.

So that winter day, we headed to the corner store wearing hoodies. (This was long before the Trayvon Martin incident, so there was nothing sinister about guys in hoodies.) We walked back to the beer cooler, and I took three cases and passed them out. My friend said, "I can't do it." I looked him in the eye and informed him it was too late to back out and gave him the case. He took it reluctantly, and we walked calmly past the counter and straight to the door.

Once we reached the door, we broke out like runaway slaves. I could hear this Arab guy screaming, "Stop! Hold it!" at the top of his lungs while giving chase. All of a sudden, I hear a loud thud followed by a grunt and the sound of Budweiser cans bursting as they fell to the ground. The friend who had gotten cold feet fell, but luckily he was able to gather himself and make it to the trail before being caught. I was heated at him for dropping our beer, but we quickly forgot as the party was officially on. Getting away with stealing those cases made it easy for me to think I could do more risky things to get money.

By this time, I was hanging out at the gamble spot and befriended a guy who was always a big winner. These were no ordinary dice games. I'm talking $100 bets with $100 side bets. I didn't have the money to get into such high-stakes games, but I could hang out there due to my relationship with the host. Seeing that type of cash as a college freshman made me want to be part of whatever they were doing. There came a point when I entertained the thought of making runs from my hometown back to campus for money.

Those thoughts, coupled with some other close calls I had, led me to decide to leave AAMU and return home. During my second semester I called my mom and told her I wanted to come home. She was heartbroken because she wanted me to stay, and she tried everything she could to talk me out of leaving. My cousin tried hard to talk me out of leaving and promised to look out for me no matter what. However, my mind was made up. I saw a path of limited options and knew I had to change my scenery and my thought process before I became a statistic.

No Choice

Once back in Prattville, I got another 9-to-5 at a plant that manufactured brake pads. Initially, I began working the graveyard shift and was soon promoted to the first shift. My uncle worked at the same plant and had been employed there for many years. Once I moved to the first shift, I rode to work with him every day, which was the perfect situation for me.

Before I left for AAMU, I met April. She was a friend of my sister and lived in our neighborhood. The summer before I left for school, we started a courtship that would last 25 years, as we are married today.

When I returned home from school, April and I started dating seriously. Even when I went away to college, she would write me all the time, and I would see her whenever I came home, so we never lost touch. Knowing she was there made my transition home easier, as I was eager to get to know her better.

However, being with April brought back some of my old bad qualities. For example, my temper returned with a vengeance. I was protective of her when we started dating, and from the moment we met, I knew I wanted to take care of her. So I became extremely jealous, which quickly led me to become angry. I argued with my sister over the smallest things concerning April, and I even became angry with my mom a few times, so much so that I would hit and break things before I even realized what I had done.

One time, I somehow got locked out of the house, and I became so angry that I punched out my bedroom window. Obviously, this did not go over well with Mom. She was so upset over it that she wanted me to leave. I ended up going to stay with my Grandmother Lizzie for a few days. While I was there, my grandmother prayed for me and talked to me about my temper. It was at that point that I knew I had to change and rid myself of that demon once and for all, or it was going to destroy me. I was able to channel my anger and redirect it positively in other areas of my life.

I worked at the plant with my uncle for over a year. Each day, I would take my lunch break with him and some of the other guys who had been employed there for over 20 years. Our lunches consisted of leftovers from the previous night's meal or potted meat, crackers, and a warm honey bun (can't forget the honey bun).

Our lunchtime conversations were always entertaining, and I enjoyed working with those guys. However, I began to wonder if there was anything else out there for me. The guys would tell me to do more with my life, and I would always listen, but I had no idea what more there was I could do.

The work at the plant was easy. I worked on a rotary saw, and my job was to cut the brake shoes into sections so they could fit onto the 18-wheelers. Working conditions weren't that great. It was incredibly hot and dusty inside the plant. At the end of each shift, you could blow your nose for hours, and black residue from the dust in the air would come out on the Kleenex.

One morning, I arrived at work at my normal time; but when I got to the front entrance, I knew something was different. There were people sitting outside at the picnic tables looking dejected. My first thought was that there had been an accident and that someone had been hurt or, even worse, killed. Later, we found out that the company had executed a large layoff, which affected the entire third shift and a number of people on the second shift.

For the moment, it didn't appear that my job was affected at all, so I proceeded to my workstation and began my day. Midway through my shift, the assistant plant manager stopped by my station and told me he needed to talk with me. While in his office he told me that due to a slow-down in business a decision was made to eliminate some shifts which affected several jobs. He assured me that my job was safe, but he needed me to move to the second shift. Initially, I thought I was lucky to have a job, so I thanked him for the continued employment and accepted the spot on the second shift.

However, as I walked back to my workstation I started to think about everything. I was comfortable with my situation on first shift, as my life was organized around those hours. I rode to work with my uncle, and he was going to continue to work first shift, so moving to a later shift wasn't the move for me.

I returned to the plant manager's office and let him know that I no longer wanted to move to second shift and that first shift was a better fit for me. He looked at me and politely said, "Herman, you do not have a choice." I will never forget how I felt when he said that to me. Here I was, 21 years old, and I was being told I didn't have a choice.

> Here I was, 21 years old, and I was being told I didn't have a choice.

I managed to get through most of my workday, but for some reason I could not get that statement out of my head. It was eating at me, and I asked myself, *If I have no choice this early in life, what does the future hold for me?*

I turned off my machine, cleaned up my workstation, and walked back to the manager's office. I took off my hardhat and safety glasses and looked him in the eye and said, "I just wanted to let you know that I do have a choice, and I choose to leave effective immediately." Given that the shift hadn't ended, I was relegated to sitting outside until my uncle finished his shift.

Before the shift ended, I was summoned to come back into the building because the head plant manager wanted to speak with me. He told me he liked my work product and offered to retain my position on the first shift, but making the choice to leave and control my own destiny empowered me like never before. It was at that moment I made the decision to further my education and do so with the same vigor and aggressiveness I had once done as an athlete.

A New Team

In the fall of 1993, I made the short drive from Prattville to the campus of Alabama State University in Montgomery. Sure, I'd been on the campus numerous times as a visitor, but I had never been there as a member of the student body.

When I arrived, I had no idea what I wanted to study. All I knew was that ASU was where I belonged. It struck me during my first year on the yard. Being at ASU was the first time I became passionate about learning. It actually felt "cool" to be considered smart. Even though I've never thought of myself as smart, it was something I was told almost daily by my instructors. The positive feedback, along with being surrounded by images of intelligent students who looked like me, had such a profound impact on my life.

Don't get me wrong. I never lacked confidence because I was raised to believe I could do anything. But there's something special about being in a place where you feel like the majority, a place where you are surrounded by so many positive images.

During my sophomore year, I took a class called African American Humanities. My instructor, Mr. Moorer, introduced me to so many wonderful things during that course. Before taking that class, the only relevant black history I had read in my high school textbooks was about the march from Selma. Once in my high school American history class, the teacher called the class to order and announced, "Today, all of my black students should sit up straight and pay attention because we will cover the Civil Rights Movement." Mind you, it was only ten or so pages out of 400 or more.

After my teacher made her announcement, I raised my hand and asked, "Shouldn't we sit up straight and pay attention every day?" For some reason, my question infuriated the teacher, and she told me to go to the office.

So going from that high school experience to my college African American Humanities course initially made me angry because I knew that black people had made many contributions to this country, but that information is not a part of the traditional high school curriculum for all students. However, my anger didn't last long. Once I started learning about Nat Turner, Frederick Douglass, The Harlem Renaissance, and many other black men and women, I felt more empowered than ever before.

It wasn't until the end of my sophomore year that I decided on a major. After two years of study, I still had no idea what my major would be. Honestly, I didn't give it much thought, after I decided I wanted nothing else to do with athletics, I never took the time to determine what my best career choice would be. Fortunately, I had guidance counselors to help me figure these things out.

Upon exiting University College, I had a meeting with my guidance counselor to declare my major. I wasn't aware of the fact that I had to declare a major, and my guidance counselor laughed and told me that since I was moving into my junior year I had to choose something. We talked about a few things, and then she asked me if I had ever thought about majoring in business—accounting, to be exact. I thought about it for a moment, and it didn't sound so bad. Rodney Zeigler, a good friend of mine from high school, said that accounting was a good major, and so my choice was made.

I'm a huge believer of fate and destiny and that some things are just meant to be. I think fate was responsible for the circumstances surrounding the selection of my first accounting course, Principles of Accounting (ACCT 214). My instructor, Dr. Jean Crawford, was the chair of the accounting department. In that same class, I would meet Terrance Turner, who would become one of my closest friends and introduced me to the rest of the guys who made up the TallaDallas crew.

Dr. Crawford was one of the most influential people I met at ASU. She was a tough instructor, but she had such a giving spirit and took a genuine interest in the lives of her students. From the time I met her in 1995 until the day I graduated, she would always say, "Mr. Moncrief, if you spent just 30 more minutes of your time each night studying . . ." Terrance and I both received A's in that accounting course, and from that day until graduation, instructors knew who we were.

On the first day of my marketing course, the instructor called my name and said, "Mr. Moncrief, I've heard really good things about you." It seems my reputation had preceded me. One may think this would have put a lot of pressure on me to live up to those expectations, but actually it was just the opposite. Instead of being intimidated by what my instructor said, I embraced it. I welcomed the notoriety, especially from an academic standpoint, and I worked hard to stay on top of things.

Given that I was late to the whole academic game, my success didn't come easy. It also proved to be a challenge since I worked my way through college all four years. During that time, I worked several different jobs in manufacturing plants and restaurants, and I even drove a Coca-Cola truck for a while. Somehow I always found time to study, no matter how late it was. It was the only way for me to keep up and maintain my GPA. In some ways I think being able to hold down a job and also juggle a major as demanding as accounting helped to prepare me for what I would encounter in my professional life.

Meeting Terrance was the beginning of my relationship with TDI (TallaDallas). It was toward the end of my first accounting course when he invited me to a party the guys were having. He said, "Man, I got this group of cats I hang out with, and we're throwing a party tonight at Red Lion Apartments. Come check us out." At the time, I didn't know TallaDallas' reputation, but I knew Terrance was a pretty cool brother, and I figured I would check out the set. That party turned out to be one of the livest campus parties I ever attended.

As I continued to meet the members of the group, there was one thing that was evident to me. These guys were all smart, and I knew this was a group I could pull from positively, so I started hanging around them more. The more of them I met the more impressed I became with the brotherhood and the vision to succeed. It's rare to see so many brothers who knew how to maintain a good balance in terms of having a good time, yet are focused on shaping their futures.

If there was a class that they had taken before me, they made sure I was prepared when I walked into that classroom, and I did the same for them. The combination of having Dr. Crawford in my corner coupled with the relationship I fostered with the members of TDI basically ensured that I would have a successful collegiate experience.

By my senior year, I had so far successfully navigated the dreaded College of Business Administration (The BA). I was 18 hours away from realizing my goal of graduating college, but there was one small problem. I needed permission from the dean of the College of Business to take an 18-hour course load, and getting that approval meant going through Dean Percy Vaughn!

Anyone who has attended The BA will tell you that Dean Vaughn was the end-all be-all in the College of Business. It started with him and ended with him. Up until that time, I had escaped being in any of his classes, primarily due to the fact that he was more of a marketing instructor and I was an accounting major. But I was determined to make this semester my last semester, so I went to his office to ask for the permission I needed to take the course load.

Once he was available to see me, I walked into his office, shook his hand, and introduced myself. Then I told him that I was 18 hours short of completing my studies and wanted to make this semester my last semester.

To explain what happened next, I have to point out that at this point in my life, I still had an ear piercing I had gotten shortly after graduating high school. So, after I finished my spiel, Dean Vaughn responded by saying, "Get the hell out of my office!" Clearly, he was joking, right?

"Are you serious?" I asked, obviously nervous.

"Hell yes, I'm serious, and don't come back to my office until you remove that earring from your ear!"

Angry but also confused, I had no other option but to leave. I headed to Dr. Crawford's office and told her what had just happened. She assured me everything would be all right, but she also said that Dean Vaughn was right about my earring and that I needed to remove it and schedule another meeting with him. I scheduled another meeting for the next day, but before I entered the dean's office, I removed my earring and put it in my pocket. It seems once the offending jewelry was removed, we were able to talk.

Dean Vaughn grilled me on how I thought I could take an 18-hour course load and told me he could bury me with 12 hours. I restated my case and told him that two of the courses were light, which would make the work easier for me to handle. He informed me that he received a call from Dr. Crawford, who had vouched for my ability to do the work. Then he granted me his permission to take the course load, but he let me know that I'd better not disappoint.

Before I left his office, Dean Vaughn told me that he had turned me away the day before in order to teach me a lesson. He asked, "Do you know how hard it will be for you to get your foot in the door somewhere when you go out into the real world?" He told me the earring should have been gone long ago and that I would be entering a professional environment where people would be looking for any small reason to weed me out, so I shouldn't give them any reason to do so.

I thanked the dean not only for his approval of my course load but also for that valuable life lesson. In a way, I left his office changed. I had entered as a college student but left as an aspiring CPA. The earring was a thing of the past because I was now on my way to bigger and better things.

A New Opportunity

I graduated cum laude with a BS in accounting from ASU in the summer of 1997. Upon graduation, I didn't have a job and was seriously considering going back to get my MBA. As with many of my friends, the lack of internship opportunities made it hard to secure a job coming out of undergrad, so continuing my education seemed like the right path for me.

I had planned to sit out the fall semester, take the GMAT, and apply to schools for the spring semester. Keidi Smith (Leach), a good friend of mine, was working as an accounts payable clerk for a local carpet retailer. We had attended ASU and graduated at the same time with degrees in accounting. She was leaving

Montgomery, and she thought I would be a good fit for her job at the carpet retailer, and asked me if I would be interested.

I was called in for an interview—well, I guess you could call it an interview. I met with the controller for about 20 minutes, and he said that Keidi had given me a glowing referral. He thought I was a sharp guy and wouldn't have any problems at all in the job. He ended the interview by asking me, "When can you start?" I'm thinking that it couldn't possibly be this easy, right? But once again, fate was on my side, so this was meant to be.

A larger retailer headquartered in Atlanta, Georgia, had recently purchased the company, so the Montgomery branch was relocating to Atlanta in January 1998. The move would work perfectly with my plans to start school in the spring. After working for a couple of months, I was asked to take on more staff accountant duties, and subsequently I was asked by the controller to join his new team in Atlanta. He knew about my plans for graduate school but indicated that I would learn a lot more in a year with him than I would in any graduate program.

At first, I was skeptical because I thought finishing my MBA was the way to go, but after several discussions, I accepted the position. This was a big role for me because after the acquisition, the controller lost his entire staff. When we relocated to Atlanta, he and I were the only ones to relocate.

This was my first job out of college. I helped interview candidates and made hiring decisions. I had my own office, and people came to me with questions. The funny thing is that I was never scared of the opportunity, as I felt well prepared for that moment. ASU gave me all the tools needed to be successful, and once I got the opportunity, I applied everything I had learned.

I worked for the Maxim Group for a year and developed a relationship with the CFO of the parent company. Over lunch, he asked me why I didn't choose a career in public accounting. He thought I had what it took to succeed in public accounting (he was a KPMG alum) and offered to make a call for me.

At that time, the company was in the midst of its annual audit, which was being performed by Arthur Andersen (AA), the well-known accounting firm. I'd encountered several AA auditors while they were performing field work, and one of the managers asked me the same question my CFO had asked about going into public accounting. I told them both the same thing. I didn't go into public accounting because of the limited internship opportunities. The AA auditing manager also offered to make a call.

I subsequently received job offers from KPMG, Arthur Andersen, and The Home Depot. Ultimately, I accepted a position with AA as staff auditor in December 1998, and my career took off from there.

Today, I am the vice president of finance for MEDHOST, Inc., located in Nashville, Tennessee. I married my long-time girlfriend, April, in 2001; and we have two wonderful kids, Bryce and Asia. I still have a lasting relationship with the brothers of TDI, and we all get together at least once a year and celebrate life. So now I can finally say that my whole crew is loungin', every day, no more public housin'!

CHAPTER TEN

MORE THAN MONEY
JEREMY SPRATLING

Planting Seeds

My dream of being a business owner became my reality after a journey through many challenges and opportunities. At times they were one and the same. Hardships are like seeds: In the right light they can grow into wisdom and strength, but when we're lost in a dark state of mind, our hardships shrivel us with bitterness and resignation. I am no stranger to hardship; but optimism, a vision for how I wanted to live, and faith in myself has made all the difference in my life.

Early one morning when I was a boy, no older than five, I was roused from bed. The adults shouted, "Stay inside! Stay inside!" and I stood at the screen door in my pajamas, just beyond the reach of autumn's early chill, the night my beloved Uncle Albert was killed right down the street from our house. This moment in my early life taught me to take nothing for granted.

Uncle Albert was the main male influence and father figure in my early childhood. He was alive and present in my world when I fell asleep, and then he was gone before the sun rose over another day in Talladega, Alabama. Losing Uncle Albert gave me first-hand knowledge that time is a precious and finite resource. That knowledge is the legacy Uncle Albert left for me.

When I was six, my mom married my stepfather, and we moved out of my grandma's house. Before I finished elementary school, however, I watched my mother bury my baby sister, Tina. At the funeral, they let me see her body as she lay in a white casket. She was dressed in a white gown and cap and was so very small.

When I saw Tina for the last time, I saw my mom cry for the first time, and from my mom's pain I sensed the magnitude of loss. I was too young to understand the depth of my mom's pain, but I was stoic and strong for her because I thought that's what she needed from me. Watching Mom lose Tina taught me to recognize grief and offer empathy to others. This is a gift I treasure to this day. Losing my sister reminded me once again that life is too short, and our time here with our loved ones is precious.

Watching Mom lose Tina taught me to recognize grief and offer empathy to others.

Wise use of my time was also important to me as I endured several surgeries for a congenital digestive disorder while still a small boy. My mom and grandma sheltered me, as I was too small to keep up with boys my age, but I always occupied my time.

Whenever I could I enjoyed the happy atmosphere of my cousins' more traditional families. My uncles John and Rufus worked hard to lead stable households, and I valued that stability. I appreciated knowing that the same toys would be there when I visited and that I would find good food instead of tension in their welcoming homes. Their families were a sort of oasis from the hardships of my health issues and personal losses.

My mother had two more daughters with my stepfather, and at times things were tight. Until I was 15, the five of us lived in a single-wide trailer; and during some winters, we relied on kerosene heat and extra blankets to stay warm. Food was scarce and never wasted. When something broke, my stepfather had to fix it or find someone who could help him fix it.

Watching my mom and stepfather negotiate difficult circumstances taught me the art of bartering and that money is not the only form of currency in life. From the strong example set by my uncles and the struggles in my own home, I learned that security and peace, as well as skills and flexibility, all have a value beyond dollars.

As I got older, I recovered from my early childhood illness and became a strong young man. I played the trumpet and the baritone and enjoyed adventures in the woods that surrounded our neighborhood.

In those same woods, a friend and I came across a box of inspirational booklets and envelopes. Most 12-year-old boys would probably leave the box where they found it, but I put each booklet in an envelope and sold them door-to-door. I sold every last booklet and saw how opportunity can only lead to success when I got up and followed it. Growing up without material comforts made me want to work, so I cut yards and raked leaves. When I was 16, I started my first paying job washing dishes at Quincy's Restaurant.

I worked my way up to hot-bar cook at Quincy's while participating in sports and music in high school. I was too busy enjoying my life to get in any trouble, but suddenly high school was over and I was adrift. I immediately tried to enlist in the United States Air Force, but my enlistment was waived after I received a music scholarship to Alabama State University. Instead of the Air Force, I joined the National Guard to help with my college expenses.

Just as in high school, I worked hard in college. One of my roommates at ASU connected me with a job at Morrison's Cafeteria. I had more than three years of restaurant experience, but at Morrison's I went in at 9:00 A.M. and didn't get off until 9:00 P.M. every weekend.

It Has to Get Better

I came home to my roommates, exhausted and facing schoolwork, while they were preparing for a night on the town. While my best friends were enjoying their youth, I was getting burned by hot food, and my skin and clothes were covered in a film of grease. It took days for the smell to wash away, only for the weekend to come and start it all over again. I'd had enough of working my way up in a one-floor industry with no opportunities.

Even though I wasn't certain what I wanted to do with my life, I had to start somewhere. I started with the suit. I remembered a program on television about dressing for success, and the presenter said to look your most professional. Navy suits should be worn with gold buttons. I went shopping for such a suit, but I couldn't afford the right suit, so I had to find another way.

At J. Riggen's, I bought a plain blue suit. Then I bought a package of gold buttons at Walmart. Back in high school, I'd taken home economics, so I was able to sew on the gold buttons, and I hemmed the pants.

That Monday, I went to every bank, commercial building, and office park and applied for any available job. Because of my efforts, I landed a job as a part-time bank teller. This was the moment my business career and climb upward began, and I was happy to give notice at the restaurant and move onward and upward.

Every opportunity possesses an element of risk. To enter a new room you must leave the old one, and sometimes it feels like you're leaving a sure thing. I took a leap of faith spending my hard-earned money from Morrison's on a suit with no promise of a better job, but I believed in myself. I believed I could do better. Yes, Morrison's gave me a steady paycheck, but at what price? Was their money worth what I was losing?

I was a young man, and young men often mistakenly believe that money is finite and time is infinite, while the reverse is true. Between Quincy's and Morrison's, I'd learned everything I was going to learn as line cook, and I left that business with a love of cooking; but I also had the wisdom and confidence never to limit my potential.

If I'd been too afraid to give up my job at Morrison's, I might be there all these years later without even being promoted to general manager. I kept my head up and looked beyond my immediate need to see the restaurant business for what it was and what opportunities it held for someone like me, and I knew I wasn't in the right place.

Although I was wise enough to wait until I had a new job lined up before I quit Morrison's, I wasn't afraid to invest in that suit and pursue the right opportunity for myself. I could have angrily quit in protest to how terrible the conditions were at that job with no next step in mind. Instead, I let that bad experience inspire me to imagine what I could become and make that happen.

My new job as a teller brought new opportunities, and I advanced to full-time employment at the bank. Because of my schedule, I left Alabama State and continued my education at Auburn University at Montgomery. The class availability at Auburn worked better with my work obligations, enabling me to grow my career, even as I completed my college coursework and eventually graduated from Auburn with a BS in economics.

Education Gives You a Path

Education has always mattered to me. My grandma not only preached the value of education, but she also practiced what she preached and set an example for all of us. Grandma didn't have the opportunity to complete high school when she was a young girl or when she was the young mother of eight children and working in a middle-school cafeteria. Yet she never gave up on her dream of education and returned to school in her fifties to earn her high school diploma. She continued her education by taking courses that interested her at the local community college and strengthened her mind through constant reading.

Though I lost Grandma three years ago, and I miss her every day, her legacy is ingrained in me. The importance of education is a value I share with my own young children and through my work with Turning Dreams Into Realities. This is how I honor her spirit and tenacity.

I continued my own education and then earned my master's degree from the Graduate School of Banking at LSU and pursued many professional designations, training classes, and certificates as a commercial banker. Just because you have eaten a meal doesn't mean you're finished eating for the rest of your life.

Education is like that, and college is not a short-term goal but the jumping off point for a life of gaining knowledge and professional skills and developing strength of character. Education nourishes the mind and is an investment in yourself. It doesn't simply open doors; it gives you the confidence to walk through them.

My mom always says, "Have a plan. Work the plan." Plans are tactical methods and a strategy to achieve your dreams; and like all tactics, you need to modify, adapt, and adjust to circumstances. Flexibility is required to work a plan.

I never abandoned my vision or my plan in response to a setback. I'm inspired by what Martin Luther King Jr. said about accepting finite disappointment but never losing infinite hope. Instead of giving up my dream, I worked my plan to move me forward through the circumstances I faced. Following any dream means dealing with reality. So I never surrendered my dream. I just modified my plan.

Sometimes in life my dream was just a direction toward something I couldn't yet define, so I headed in the right direction but encountered detours along the way. When I've been diverted by circumstances, I make the most of it.

Ultimately, I was offered two jobs in banking—one in Montgomery, Alabama, and the other in Nashville, Tennessee. Neither of those options felt like the right fit for me, so I trusted that I knew who I was and what was right for me. I didn't take the opportunity just because it was there. Instead, I was patient and true to myself and discovered my next opportunity, and the next, and the next after that. I kept working my plan by improving my circumstances and my mind. I always thought two steps ahead of my competition throughout my career, and this prepared me to recognize and take advantage of opportunities and create new ones for myself.

The most important thing I know is my own nature. I've always been self-aware enough to know who I was in the moment and remain driven to become the person I want to be. Though I still enjoy cooking, I knew I was unhappy doing it for my paycheck and that it wasn't my dream or my future. Likewise, I enjoyed a long and prosperous career in commercial banking where I learned many skills and had gratifying successes.

Still, I knew in my heart I needed to feel the liberation of owning my own business. I wanted a stronger grip on my destiny. Here I was later in life but still young, facing another opportunity that involved risk. I deliberated giving up a comfortable situation to pursue my dream.

I talked to my mom about the risks and rewards of following my passion and starting my own business. Mom is tough and never says anything she doesn't mean. Her childhood nickname was Big Red, and if her sisters had a problem, they got Big Red to handle it for them. I learned toughness from her. She taught me never to just quit but to always have a plan. Mom always preached business ownership and taught me never to be afraid to take a chance, because as she says, "Nothing fails but a try."

> "There is no shortcut to achievement. Life requires thorough preparation."

Before I left banking to start my business, Mom told me what she always says, "Have a plan, then work the plan," and I took her advice because no one has my best interests in her heart more than my mom. She's my rock, and I can always rely on her to remind me to trust myself.

George Washington Carver said, "There is no shortcut to achievement. Life requires thorough preparation." Before I launched my business, I first explored my experience helping hundreds of clients launch their own successful ventures over the years. I pulled together all that I'd learned in life and made a strong plan to create my corporate facilities management business. I took my time and built a strong business plan. Then I trusted my business acumen and experience and took the leap. Eighteen months later, my dream became my reality, and I left banking to run my own company.

Just as there's no such thing in life as instant success, there is also no such thing as permanent success. Success is sustained by vigilance and effort. Just because you got out of the harbor doesn't mean you can stop steering the ship. I have a plan for my sustained success and personal happiness in life, but I have to keep working the plan.

During the recession, the real-estate part of my business, like so many other businesses and families, was affected by the housing bubble. I took the economic impact seriously, but I took it in stride. I used the tools I had to revise my plan, but I stuck to the business fundamentals that have always served me well. I weathered that storm, accounted for the losses, and today my business continues to flourish.

Opportunity comes when you look beneath the surface. I've landed big accounts just by showing up, listening, and seeing the need firsthand. If I can see what a client needs, I can demonstrate how we can help them and then make that happen. Sometimes I do have to decline, but I showed that client respect and gave that person my time. I never walk away from a situation like that without learning something and creating a new connection. Even if it's not the right situation for me, I never have to wonder that I've passed by an unseen opportunity because I didn't bother to look.

Nothing compares to the pride and freedom of owning my own business. Every day, I feel assured I am investing my time and energy in my own creation and influencing my future and my children's future through my efforts. My dream includes being the best father a man can be, and to do that I have to be present and available to my children, even as I work hard for their future.

I met my own dad for the first time when I was 36 years old. I internalized what kind of father I would like to be, and that became part of my plan. As a boy and a young man, I always told myself that if I had children, they would know their father.

I do indulge my children in ways that I could not be indulged myself. I give things and opportunities to my kids that not every child is as fortunate to have, but that is my prerogative to use my success to enjoy those experiences with my children. I set an example for them by doing what I love every day and working hard at it.

My children are so proud of their dad, the business owner who sponsors their athletic teams and lets them run around his office. I have a passion for doing business, closing deals, and seeing the manifestation of my efforts in the business I've created. When you're self-employed, you own your time; and when you love what you do, it doesn't feel like work.

I'm living my dream today, but my life is no fairytale. I didn't get here through magic but through vision and hard work, and my life is still a work in progress. I've been discouraged before, for example, when I couldn't get in the door at a big investment firm. However, I've also been flexible and made the best of the hand I've been dealt in life.

I was devastated by the loss of Uncle Albert and my extraordinary grandma, but I've also honored them by appreciating the time given to me and nourishing my mind with education. My work with Turning Dreams Into Realities is how I give back to Grandma, Mom, and my uncles who helped me become the man I am.

My advice to young people faced with hardship and challenge is some of the oldest advice known to mankind: Know yourself. Know who you are and always believe in yourself. It is the only way to become the person you want to be.

Trust your intelligence and trust your instincts, but don't be afraid to ask for advice. Success is something sustained through small steps and huge leaps of faith. The small steps are all the hard jobs and long hours you will have to work to get ahead. The leaps of faith happen when you have a plan and sufficient faith in yourself to work that plan. First, however, you must invest in yourself.

Knowing what you want to do is one thing; knowing what you don't want to do is another and is just as important. I was good at restaurant work, and when I was starting out I enjoyed it. Yet over time, I grew, and the job did not grow with me. Not only is it acceptable to outgrow a position, it's a sign of success that you have mastered one thing and that it's time to find a new opportunity. There is a balance in life, and you should never be too proud to work a job with limited rewards or be too scared to leave that job for something that's not simply "better" but is better for you. Only you can decide that for yourself.

There's no shame at age 18 or 25 not knowing exactly what you want to be doing when you're 40 or 50 years old. When you're young, invest your time and energy in discovering what you love to do. Find your direction, and be true to that compass. Faith in yourself and your vision is necessary to persevere through all the small steps and hard work. Faith in yourself is also necessary to fuel the courage required to take those big leaps toward your dreams.

Maybe you weren't so lucky to have that strong family background, and you have to keep believing in yourself without that support. Maybe you don't have an educated family, but surely there are strengths and weaknesses in all the people you know. Learn from those examples, and let those lessons inform the person you are and the person you want to become. If you can bear to examine the difficult moments in your life in the right light, you will see that you were always strong and that your struggles only made you stronger. That extra strength is an advantage that only comes to those who overcome adversity.

Where there are deficiencies in your life, take strength from the people around you. Surround yourself with positive people, and avoid negative people. Negative people aren't your friends; they drain your energy and undermine your vision. Negative people and negative messages poison your vision. Don't focus on what you don't have right now; focus on what you are going to do to make your life what you want it to be.

Positive people want you to succeed and will help you. The value of positive friends is endless. Sometimes their encouragement or a favor at the right moment makes all the difference on your journey. Back at Alabama State, I made 11 friends. This was over 20 years ago, and the 12 of us are still great friends.

We came from different cities and different families, but we became a community based on friendship and optimism.

We refused to let one another fail because we believed in each man's potential and supported each man's dreams. It is this priceless and selfless support that drives Turning Dreams Into Realities (TDI).

Life can't be easy for anyone, but the 12 of us are committed to help other college students avoid the pitfalls and avoidable struggles we each endured. We mentor young men and provide financial assistance and guidance not simply because we can but because it's the right thing to do. We want our beneficiaries to have and to seek people in their lives who won't let them give up on their vision or themselves, and when they are struggling we will help them find opportunities to exercise faith in themselves.

Want Some Advice?

You must allow people to help you. When I was 16, my great-uncle John taught me that my time had more value than I was giving it. He taught me to see and demand what I am worth.

Uncle John did this by inviting me to work for his construction and masonry business one long week in Atlanta, Georgia. I hauled bricks and bags of cement through the long summer days. At the end of the week, I was tired and sweaty, and Uncle John came to me and asked what he owed me. I didn't know what a week of my labor was worth, so I told him to decide.

Uncle John gave me $20 and a box of Crunch & Munch for five sweltering days of hard work in the sun, and that's how I learned to set my own value and to value my time. Uncle John knew I was worth more than that, and he wanted me to know it. When people reach out to help you learn hard lessons in a week instead of a lifetime, it's wise to listen and to learn.

When you are young with so few years behind you and so many ahead, it may seem like you have far more time than money; but don't throw your time at money. Money can be reclaimed; but once time has passed, it is gone forever, so invest your time well while its still in abundance.

Many people say, "Time is money," and while you can measure time in dollars earned, time is a currency so much more precious than dollars. Time is a finite resource, and success in life is not simply accumulating money. A man's wealth is the result of well-invested time in one's self and one's relationships. The well-invested time pays you back with faith in yourself, strength of character, and a well-lived life. Don't waste your time working hard for the wrong things or the wrong reasons.

After some time in life, you might find yourself generating a good income and living a nice lifestyle and still not feel you're going where you want to go or becoming who you could be. Don't trap yourself in a career you don't like just for money. Find or make an opportunity with momentum. Never give up, and never stop looking for and creating new opportunities. Have a plan, and work toward that plan, but be flexible enough to take the steps necessary to keep moving. Dreams are not a point on the horizon. They are the horizon.

Interacting with other people creates opportunities for you and for them. Every person is part of a chain of people who are lifted and lift one another in return. Take advantage of help, but never take it for granted. Be gracious, and forge your character into a strong link that helps lift those who follow you. Money and time have limits. A wealth of character is a resource that can never be exhausted, and it is strengthened by your relationships.

I rarely have regrets in life; but if I could go back to when I was young, I would connect with more people. I would have been in less of a hurry to "get ahead," and I would have given some of my time and attention to the people around me. There were classmates and coworkers who've drifted away in life, and I wish I'd invested the time in getting to know them better and strengthening and extending my community.

Yes, I have many old and dear friends, but a man can never have too many friends. The stronger your community, the further you can take one another toward your goals and dreams.

Some days the hardest thing will be to keep your faith in yourself, but it is also the most fundamental part of success. If you don't trust yourself or your dream, it shows. Everyone has doubts. The key to doubt is to evaluate what it can teach you and then move out of its shadow. Have faith in your worth.

When you engage in activities that are meaningful to you, the harmony it brings provides more security and peace than money. Follow the path of your passions, and success will follow you.

Take something positive from every experience in your life, and take nothing for granted. This world is not perfect and can provide you with an endless number of reasons to be hurt and angry.

Fredrick Douglass once said, "We have to do with the past only as we can make it useful to the present and the future." The power to take the best lessons from the past and set aside the bad comes from your vision and your commitment to your future.

You cannot move forward if you're stuck in the past.

To reach your dreams, you never have to be the best in the world, just the best that you can be in the moment. You just need to live every moment to the best of your ability and continuously become the best version of yourself you can manage.

You have the power to see the world as a burden or an opportunity. Either way, you have to exist in this world; but when you see the possibilities, you will gravitate toward something bigger and better.

My grandma and my mom taught me to be honest and to have high integrity. My large family set the example to do the right thing, no matter how hard it is. That honesty and integrity starts with you, and remember how far you've come each step of the way and that there were people who helped make your journey smoother.

Yet, years from now, when I am done with this business and when this part of my dream comes to a close, I will gladly let it go to my children. My children are my legacy, and the most important thing I leave for them will not be my corporate facilities management business or even pride that I was a successful businessman or community leader. My gift to my children is worth much more than a company or a trust fund.

Head High. Eyes Front!

When my children come of age to inherit the business I worked so hard to create, they can sell it, dismantle it, run it, or be rid of it because it was my dream not theirs. My most precious gift to my children is the spirit and faith to follow their own dreams. What I will pass to my children and the people who remember me at the end of my days is nothing so temporary as money, but the values and lessons I inherited myself.

I will leave my children a legacy of tenacity and intellectual curiosity that I inherited from my grandmother. I will leave them the ambition, humility, hope, self-respect, and work ethic I inherited from my uncles. My children will also inherit the values of generosity, reverence, and joyfulness given to me by my community of friends and colleagues. I will pass to them the perseverance and wisdom my mother gave me. All of these things were poured into me; and I used them to strengthen my own attributes of vision, aspiration, intelligence, kindness, and self-confidence.

I would not have achieved all that I have in my life without the people and lessons who have influenced me over the years. Yet at this moment and when my life ends, everything I am and everything I've accomplished required me to stay true to myself.

A million people can love you and tell you you're worthy of your dreams, but if you don't believe it, your dreams will always be impossible. You must believe in yourself and believe that life is more than things. It's more than clothes, cars, money, or homes. Life is the accumulation of time, thought, community and connection, love, and commitment to something larger than a single man. None of us is alone in the world, but each of us has the responsibility to choose where we want to go and how we will treat the people we meet along the way.

You may call me a wealthy man, but my wealth in life is not from the money I made but from what I have made of myself.

I invested in my friendships, my education, my family, and my dreams. Yes, all of those things gave me material success, but it also gave me that one thing we all know money doesn't buy. I pursued my happiness in life, I found it, and I treasure and protect it. That is my American Dream.

Right now, you have everything it takes to chase the horizon and move toward your dream. No one can stop you from making it your own.

CHAPTER ELEVEN

WENT FROM NEGATIVE TO POSITIVE
DEMETRICE JONES

I grew up in Talladega, Alabama, and through the eyes of a child, everything appeared innocent and without worry. However, those moments would prove to be short-lived.

My parents were married in May 1969, and my mother later gave birth to three children. Though most of my memories of that time are vague, I'm reminded of my childhood when I visit my parents in the house where I was raised and thumb through the pages of the old photo album. I recall a story that my mother, Lillie Jones, told me when I was just a teenager.

It was midday, and I was a newborn baby sound asleep in a single-wide trailer in a small community barely inside the Talladega, Alabama, city limits. Because we did not have an electric clothes dryer in the trailer, my mother went out the back door to make sure the laundry was dry on the clothesline. My older brother, Walter Jr., completely capable of getting around on his own, trailed close behind while my mother held my sister Amanda's hand as she stumbled along beside her.

My mother quickly pulled the clothes from the line and made her way back inside. In the corner of the living room, only a few feet from where I was asleep, she noticed something that appeared to be a necktie on the floor. Not giving it much thought, she moved closer to the object when she suddenly realized it was a snake. Terrified of snakes, my mother quickly grabbed my sister in one arm, pulled my brother with the other, and then ran back outside.

In her attempt to go back inside, Mom noticed that the snake had slithered closer toward my crib, perhaps targeting the milk in the bottle. At that moment, she was frozen with fear and couldn't force herself to go back inside. Fortunately, a neighbor was nearby and ran inside and pulled me from the baby crib.

My mother was 25 years old and shared parental responsibilities with my father to raise their three young children in the best environment possible. My father, Walter Jones Sr., was a hard worker, and this incident pushed him to work around the clock to earn enough income to build our first house.

It took only a year to construct the house, and we became new residents of the Southside community. For most of my early childhood, it was rare that my parents would let me or my siblings go outside the chain-linked fence that surrounded our house, so my circle of friends only stretched as far as the neighbors on the other side of our property line.

As each day passed, I felt different. That fence made me feel as though I lived inside an isolated bubble. The other kids would stand outside the gate that surrounded our house as I played Ping-Pong with my siblings. I didn't understand why I couldn't engage in activities with some of the other kids who roamed the neighborhood. I enjoyed the time I spent with my siblings, but the same daily routine got old. As I grew older, I began to take chances.

I finally escaped the bubble and ventured out into the neighborhood with Terrance Turner. This is what I had been waiting for—at least that's what I thought. Terrance had earned respect in the neighborhood and knew the other kids beyond just seeing them at school. However, I was pretty much an outcast in my own community. It took some time to adjust, but I was able to fit in by demonstrating some of the same interests as the other kids.

Eventually, I came to terms with the misconception my peers had of me before they got to know me. Since my father was a respected pastor, some of the kids thought I was a choirboy. I had my share of trouble like any other kid, and to some degree my actions were far worse than theirs. On the one hand, I admired my father as well as the valuable things he taught me along the way. On the other hand, I believed that I needed to find a way to separate myself from this "choirboy" image, but I didn't have a clue where to start.

As I look back on my junior high and high school experiences, it was apparent that academics were not my main focus. Mostly, I looked forward to the dismissal bell so I could hurry home to play video games or play basketball with friends in my backyard.

My grades fell well south of average. It wasn't because I couldn't learn; I just didn't have the motivation to apply myself. So it was no secret on how I spent my summer days. While my peers were out enjoying fun in the sun, I was spending my valuable hours of the day in summer school. That was the price I had to pay for neglecting to take care of business during the normal school year.

I had no realistic goals established and no clear vision.

I had no realistic goals established and no clear vision. Many of the decisions I made were ill-advised. My parents constantly stayed on me about my academic progress and stressed that a good education was an essential key to success. My father wanted more insight about my academic achievement, so he took a more hands-on approach. He gave me clear instructions on what he wanted done.

I was given a folder that I would present to each of my teachers in order to document my academic progress, as well as my behavior in their classroom. This was not good. What this meant was that I could no longer go home with the notion that I didn't have any homework or didn't cause any disruption in class. My teachers documented everything! In most cases, bringing the folder home to my father had more repercussions than bringing home my report card at the end of the six-week term. *Where did he come up with this ridiculous concept?* I thought sarcastically.

My mother was employed with the Talladega County Board of Education and frequently substituted at Talladega High School. One of the most awkward experiences of my high school journey was to have my mother substitute for one of my classes. For her, it was just what the doctor ordered, because she knew that my chances for getting out of line were zero to none. While she was there, I couldn't carry on with my normal antics, and my classmates knew it. They made it difficult for me to get through that class period, but it was all in fun, and I would live to goof off another day. Nevertheless, those experiences reshaped my position on education, and it made me more accountable.

Ultimately, I had to pull away from the group of students that would typically take things lightly. My father's involvement, along with my mother's routine conferences with teachers, helped me to establish a more promising pathway to succeed through high school.

There were two community programs I participated in when I was growing up—Upward Bound and My Child With a Future (MCWAF). Upward Bound presented an environment that provided educational resources as well as extracurricular activities. It gave school-age kids the opportunity to engage in a productive program while on summer break. The program was an interesting pastime, and as a reward for completing it, we went to Six Flags Over Georgia, which was always the highlight.

MCWAF offered open discussion that covered topics on the key to success. The platform was well structured, and a senior member of a well-known church in Talladega oversaw the program. The integrity of MCWAF was held together by strict guidelines: We had to be punctual; but there was to be no drugs, no alcohol, and no premarital sex. Another requirement was that each member had to maintain a C or above grade point average.

About ten to fifteen teenagers, male and female, made up the group. They all appeared to be members of this church and attended services frequently. Terrance would periodically mention the program and cut short basketball games in the community to go and attend the meetings. I wanted to know more about the program, not so much for the topics of discussion, but rather the girls and the all-expense-paid adventures they would always go on.

I'm almost certain I was the only non-church member in the organization. However, I was voted in mainly because of my mischievous character, not by an overwhelming majority. Nevertheless, I began to learn many things that are relevant to my life today.

A mock board of executives was established, and we held meetings, several of which were highly intense. Apparently, there was a breakdown at some point, and the program didn't survive. It wasn't because it was unproductive. Actually, that entire experience taught me to respect others' opinions without jeopardizing a friendship or future working relationships. MCWAF, as I knew it, served its purpose.

Life Is Not a Game

In 1991, I was preparing to graduate, and it was a blessing that I had made it to this point. Despite my late run to improve my grades, it was obvious I wasn't among the top of the graduating class. To be exact, I was among the bottom of the class, ranking 188 out of 204 students, with only a half credit to spare.

However, once I graduated, I was ready to embark on life. My grade point average was far from where it needed to be to attend a four-year college or university. I didn't have a plan in place, but my father did.

The day after graduation, he took me to a local grocery store. He called for the manager, and in his bold words, he said, "This is my son, Demetrice Jones, and we need to put him to work today." The manager put his right hand under his chin and the other across his stomach and began to think. I don't know what his thoughts were, but mine were, *Isn't there an application and a formal interview process that should be involved?* Nevertheless, the manager asked if I could stock shelves. I don't remember having a chance to answer his question. All I heard from my father was, "When can he start?"

Now getting the job was cool, but what came next was life-altering. The manager said I needed to report to work at 11:45 P.M. on Sunday. He said that the night crew usually got started around midnight, and the work hours would continue through the morning—anywhere from 7:00 to 8:00 A.M. I went into a momentary daze, thinking to myself, *That's skating rink night!*

Talladega didn't have many places for activities, but Skate City was at the top of the list. Back then, we would move from the skating rink to the parking lot of the grocery store (where I was supposed to start work). Obviously, the idea didn't sit well with me, but I had to take responsibility and go to work.

I was busting it on the night-stock crew for the first four hours of my shift. The on-duty supervisor crossed my aisle, slowly approached me, and said, "You're in the real world now; you're going to have to pick up the pace!" I was only a few hours in and still learning the technique of slicing the boxes open with the box-cutter, but this supervisor was not letting up. He had the demeanor and attitude of a drill sergeant.

I was beside myself and wondering what was this thing called life. If I wanted a drill sergeant, I would have enlisted in the armed forces.

My hat was off to the other employees because they had this method down to a science and were stocking the shelves like clockwork. Unfortunately, I only lasted in the position for three days, and it didn't help that the night-crew supervisor blurted out absurd comments throughout the night. I'm not sure what his problem was. Maybe he was just trying to put on the pressure to get more production from me. Either way, it didn't work.

That morning after I clocked out, I was done. I was convinced that the grocery store was not the place for me! I wasn't going back—at least, that's what I thought. I wasn't quite out of the woods yet. The phone rang at home, and my father answered. It was the hiring manager inquiring about my whereabouts and why I had not shown up for work. I wasn't at home at the time. I came home in the wee hours of the night.

Early the next morning, my father took me back to the grocery store and convinced the manager to move me into another position, preferably with day hours. I was wondering how many chances I would get at this store.

They moved me to bag boy, but I only lasted two days. I worked a total of five days with that company. My father put his reputation on the line in an effort to keep me busy and productive. I felt as though I had let him down in his attempt to instill a sense of responsibility in me.

Pathway to College

The next year, I turned 19 and learned that I would become a father. I was hardly prepared to care for a child. I needed to put myself in a position to provide for my future daughter with the best life possible, just as my parents had done for me.

Attending a four-year college or university was a stretch, but I was determined to make it happen. I attended a community college in Childersburg, Alabama, in order to earn enough credits to eventually qualify to attend a four-year college program. In the meantime, I cut hair to keep cash in my pocket and to share the responsibility of raising my daughter.

I spent a lot of time straddling the fence while still trying to figure things out. I was in an all-out battle between good and evil. I adapted to the reckless lifestyle; and though I wasn't affiliated with any gangs, I often ran with a clique that was notorious for fights and trouble. I wanted the best of both worlds, and a couple of peer groups showed me both sides.

Every day after class, I had a lot of idle time on my hands. I had several groups of friends, and aside from attending community college and cutting hair, I would hang out with them periodically. A few of my friends were still in high school, and others had gone away to college. That left me to interact with those who didn't have jobs or who weren't doing anything productive, which was a recipe for disaster.

It was imperative that I separate myself from situations that eventually caused me to have run-ins with the law. I was influenced by both peer groups—some positive, others negative. I couldn't mix the two because it backfired, and now I was facing some tough decisions.

The momentary satisfaction of living on the edge was going nowhere fast. I had goals and responsibilities at this point, and there was no room for me to pay a debt to society.

I was convinced that I needed to focus more on a positive image.

My high school classmate Tyrish Garrett was home from Alabama State University (ASU) for the summer. We met up and started talking about life and all the opportunities that were before us. By the end of our conversation, I was convinced that I needed to focus more on a positive image. I had completed two years of core courses at the community college and was now eligible to attend a four-year college.

Hands down, ASU was at the top of the list. Not only was I intrigued by the annual Birmingham Magic City Classic, which I had attended over the years as a teenager, I would be surrounded by hometown friends and assured a great education. That same year, several of my other friends who had recently graduated high school applied and were all accepted at ASU. I applied, and the application was well on its way. I actually met the mail carrier at the mailbox every day in anticipation of the delivery of a response letter from ASU. If I got accepted, that would be huge for me and for my family.

The time had finally come. I held in my hand the letter that could very well determine my path in life. I opened the envelope and learned that I had been accepted to ASU and would be attending beginning the fall semester of 1993.

College

My college experience was epic, and I began to dream of success. I left behind a family in Talladega and gained a new family of friends in Montgomery. I was grateful to reconnect with classmates who were already at ASU. They gave us insight on what to expect and information on housing if we later chose to move off campus.

After settling into the new lifestyle, I was introduced to a few students who were from Texas. These were some down-to-earth guys. Our personalities immediately clicked, and we didn't waste any time as we started to engage in numerous social events and activities. We encouraged one another, and it was rare to see one member of the group without seeing another.

We bonded and did nearly everything together. We scheduled classes, met for lunch, partied, and socialized in one another's dorm rooms. As a result, TallaDallas was formed, and great things began to emerge. TallaDallas is a combination of *Talladega* and *Dallas*, representing the places we're from.

I'm grateful to be associated with such a good group of guys. Each of these members has inspired me in various ways and has played an important role in me achieving my goals. I think back on the time when college was not on my radar, but God set a pathway and surrounded me with great people.

Through my life accomplishments, I have earned a bachelor's degree in criminal justice and a master's degree in general counseling. I'm currently employed as part of the management team for a financial institution in Montgomery. In 2008 and 2009, I wrote and published two relationship novels.

I appreciate the lessons learned as I matured into an adult. Those lessons helped me understand the needs of others who shared similar circumstances. For several years, I had the privilege to work as a behavior therapist for an organization that assists at-risk students and their families achieve their goals. As a youth struggling to find my place in life, it was a personal obligation for me to reach out and provide helpful services in order to impact children and families in a positive way.

I have a beautiful family that stems from my parents and siblings to my children—Takia, Desmond, and Davious. Their show of support is undeniable, and their continuous expression of love is what has shaped me today. I thank my parents for providing me with a solid foundation and the mindset never to give up on anyone or any situation. My parents always encouraged me to pray and to put God first because He will see me through.

CHAPTER TWELVE

WORDS FROM THE MENTEES

Cornelius Warmack

I am a mentee for Turning Dreams Into Realities. I was born and raised in Union Spring, a small town in Alabama. My mother and late grandmother helped raised me. I have two brothers, two uncles, and two nieces. I graduated from Bullock County High School in the spring of 2009. When I finished high school, I worked with my mother and brother at Wayne Farms LLC. I processed chickens for restaurants all over the country. It was a hard job, and the work environment was difficult because we worked in freezing temperatures. Every day, I would go in at 4:30 in the afternoon, and I didn't get off until the wee hours of the morning.

In August 2009, I enrolled at H. Councill Trenholm State Technical College in Montgomery, Alabama. While I was taking classes, I was still working at Wayne Farms. I drove an hour to get to class and an hour to get to work. I did that for the first semester, and it was hard. I wanted to give up because I went through so many difficult obstacles. I wasn't getting enough sleep, and it seemed that every month I had car trouble; but I made it to the end of the semester.

After I finished Trenholm State in the fall of 2011, I enrolled at Alabama State University in the spring of 2012, but there was a problem. The school would not accept any of my credits from Trenholm State, so I had to start over as a freshman. I was disappointed, but that was not so bad. At ASU, I met new people who would help me with my journey through school. I did not have a job when I first arrived at ASU, but I was able to volunteer in the College of Business Administration.

I applied for a Turning Dreams Into Realities scholarship. I was asked by the chairperson of the computer information system's department to apply for the scholarship, and I did. Initially I was denied the scholarship, but I was accepted into the mentee's program. Later, they included me in the scholarship program and even helped to sponsor my trip to China as part of a program at ASU. I graduated in December 2015, and I am currently working at ASU as a digitizations technician.

While a part of the program, I've seen and learned so much. I've seen men graduate from ASU and become successful in their field of study. Now they are sharing their time and wisdom with their mentees so we can become just as successful as they are. They live in different states all over the country, but they always keep the friendship they built at ASU.

Diezman Ellis

It is an honor to be part of the Turning Dreams Into Realities mentorship/scholarship program. This program has provided me with financial support and guidance. The funding has helped me buy textbooks and other resources needed for my classes. Most college students have issues with having enough money for textbooks, and the textbooks for courses in the College of Business Administration are expensive. The check I receive each semester helps me to buy the necessary resources so I can stay ahead.

Although I was a recipient of the Alabama State Incentive Scholarship, it only covered the cost of my tuition, not my books. After buying my books and other supplies, sometimes I have little money left over to buy the other things I need. I have received other scholarship opportunities because of having scholarships I've received listed on my resume.

The mentorship aspect of this program has also allowed me to participate in an internship. One of the mentors of TDI provided me with a summer internship. I was one of the two TDI scholarship recipients who were fortunate enough to get this work experience. I worked with Mr. Jeremy Spratling in Montgomery. Sean, the other recipient, worked in Atlanta, Georgia. I was excited to receive the internship at Corporate Facilities Management. It was a great experience working with Mr. Spratling and learning how to run a small business. That internship has helped to build my resume. I was also able to make a business plan and create the guidelines for a scholarship for high school students.

In addition to the scholarship and mentorship components of TDI, I also enjoy the fellowship with the men of TDI and the other scholarship recipients. Throughout each semester, there were opportunities for everyone to meet for lunch or dinner. During these outings, our mentors would share their stories from the past. There was always good laughter, and I always feel comfortable speaking my mind and opening up to my mentors.

Periodically, my mentors have checked to see if my classes were going well and to see if there was anything I needed. I was raised by my mom, so this relationship presented a positive male role model for me and has created a bond I will never forget. I recently transferred to Auburn University where I am looking to graduate soon.

Sean Freeman

Since becoming a member of TDI a few years ago, I have grown tremendously as a young man. My mentors have taught me priceless skills and values. They don't just talk the talk; they walk the walk as well. They are completely accessible and are only a call away if I need them for anything, from advice on classes to family concerns to relationship tips.

I first joined TDI in the fall of 2012 when I met Terrence Hall and Herman Moncrief at a home football game at Alabama State University. Applying for the scholarship forced me to dig deep inside myself and look back at what I came through. The reference letter by someone who knew me also allowed me to learn and appreciate someone else's view of me. These situations have encouraged me to better myself already.

After receiving the scholarship, I participated in the organization's monthly conference calls, and a few of my mentors even took Diezman and me out to dinner. There, I was able to see that my mentors together are much like how my friends and I are with one another. That meant so much to me to see successful black men who graduated from the college I attend and who have similar backgrounds to mine. It made my dreams, along with my friends' dreams, seem that much closer to being a reality. I also liked the way they joked around and had fun, but they always put their schoolwork first.

I was blessed with the opportunity to work as an intern for Terrence at Emerson Retail Solutions. That experience changed my life because I was able to see what goes on in the big buildings that I would usually just drive by. It gave me good insight on what goes on with Fortune 500 companies and how they operate. Terrence did an excellent job of making sure I knew what was going on before he let me handle things on my own, which allowed me to do my best while I was there. Seeing how he conducted himself in the workplace and hearing the great words that his coworkers had to say about him was rewarding as well.

TDI has assisted in my growth as a person in ways that I could never imagine. I'm extremely thankful for this program and the work that my mentors put into it. TDI is about helping young men flourish as much as they can. The available resources stretch from the fields of accountancy to work in the music industry. I thoroughly enjoy my time with TDI, and I'm excited to see how big the mentorship program is growing right in front of our eyes. I recently graduated from ASU in December 2015, and I am currently looking to pursue my dreams in hotel management and entrepreneurship.

IT WAS ALL A DREAM

ABOUT THE AUTHORS

Brencleventon Donta Truss, Ed.D

Brencleveton "Donta" Truss was born in Atlanta, Georgia, but reared in Talladega, Alabama. He received his formal education at Alabama State University where he received a bachelor's, master's, and a doctorate in educational leadership, policy and law.

Currently, he is interim Vice President for Division of Student Success and Enrollment at Fort Valley State University. He is the author of *Innovation in Higher Education: An Analysis of Organizational Change and Its Role in Retaining Students*. He is involved in community activities as the past president of the Cuthbert, Georgia, Rotary Club and a proud member of Kappa Alpha Psi Fraternity, Inc.

Recently, Dr. Truss was selected and honored as one of the Best and the Brightest: Top Forty Under Forty Persons in the state of Georgia by *Georgia Trend Magazine*. Dr. Truss is also the CEO of Resource One, LLC, which is a consulting firm that focuses on helping organizations grow and operate at their most optimal level. Additionally, Resource One, LLC provides grant writing services and professional development for many educational and noneducational nonprofit agencies. On July 02, 2006, he became a licensed minister, and he is a proud husband and a busy father.

Ramone Harper

Ramone is an executive pastor and the founder of BNB Consulting and Associates, a management and consulting firm that contracts with ministries, major corporations, not-for-profits, and start-ups in the areas of business organization and development, financial management, fundraising, project management, and systems development. He is originally from Detroit, Michigan, but lived the majority of his teenage years in the Dallas-Fort Worth area.

Ramone earned his BS in public relations with a minor in business administration from Alabama State University, where he graduated summa cum laude in 1997. He is currently enrolled at Regents University, working on his master's of divinity degree. Recently, he was selected as one of the Ebony Men of the Year by the Alpha Kappa Alpha Sorority, Inc., included in the 2013-15 *Who's Who in Black Houston* publication as one of the top entrepreneurs, and honored as one of Houston's Top 50 Entrepreneurs in 2015.

He is married to his life partner, Verily, and they have four children and one grandchild.

Bryant Spencer

Bryant Spencer is a retail executive with over 18 years of merchandising and marketing experience, including strategic planning, budgeting, forecasting, and financial analysis. He is experienced in product development, private label and international brands. He grew up in Carrollton, AL. Graduated from Alabama State University with a B.S. in marketing and is obtaining his MBA from Massachusetts Institute of Technology (MIT). He and his wife Melanie currently reside in Providence, RI. Bryant is a recipient of a number of professional awards and has completed several business development courses from Northwestern's Kellogg School of Management, Notre Dame's Mendoza College of Business, and DePaul University.

Marc P. Desgraves IV

Marc is a certified public accountant with a wealth of diversified experience over multiple decades, including tax preparation, business formation and start-up services, mergers and acquisitions, Sarbanes-Oxley compliance, risk assessment, forensic accounting, internal audit, and big-four external audit. Marc currently serves as the Vice President of Risk Management for Cambium Learning Group, a publicly traded global provider of online and print solutions for the K12 education industry.

More importantly, Marc is proud of his civic contributions, which include providing numerous tax services on a pro bono basis as well as volunteering his time through organizations such as the National Association of Black Accountants and serving on the board of directors for charter schools.

In his personal time, Marc enjoys playing basketball, tackling home projects, and mentoring young people through organizations such as Big Brothers, Big Sisters or coaching youth sports.

Tyrish Garrett

Tyrish Garrett was born in Talladega, Alabama, the son of Brenda Garrett and Howard Leonard. He received his formal education at Alabama State University where he received a bachelor's of science in marketing. Tyrish, also received his M.B.A. from Troy State University in business administration. Tyrish has been employed by United Parcel Service for the last sixteen years. He has worked as the sales/marketing supervisor for the last five years. Tyrish's duties include implementation of sales strategies, evaluation of customer compliance and value, and cross-functional support for profitable sales growth. Tyrish was previously a finance supervisor with duties that included district profitability analysis, customer profitability, and auditor training.

Tyrish has served as a volunteer for United Way where he was responsible for meeting with company coordinators to plan, organize, and schedule employee meetings and assist with developing campaign goals.

Terrence Hall

Terrence Hall is originally from Talladega, Alabama. He enrolled at Alabama State University in the fall of 1993 and majored in business administration with a concentration in finance. After college, he worked as a loan processor for Northeastern Financial Services and a loan officer for Regions Financial Corporation. He was then employed with Delta Airlines, the premier airline in the global airline industry, where he worked in global sales support and services. Afterward, he worked as a learning support trainer, and he traveled extensively, domestically and internationally, to implement new policies and procedures to employees. At Delta, he was awarded with the Certificate of Excellence for outstanding performance; was a four-time member of the renowned Pinnacle Club; and a nominee for the Chairman's Club, which is the highest award to an employee with Delta Airlines.

He has now started his own tutorial service, F.I.N.A.O. (Failure Is Not An Option), that mentors youth of all ages to encourage the advocacy of good grades. He's also an independent business owner of Total Life Changes, a health and wellness organization.

Terrence is a member of Shady Grove Baptist Church where he serves as a Crusaders counselor. He is currently in a relationship and is a renowned member of Alpha Phi Alpha Fraternity, Inc.

Terrance Turner, CPA

Terrance is from Talladega, AL. He attended Alabama State University from 1993 to 1997. Terrance graduated with honors from ASU in 1997 with a B.S. in Accounting. After which, Terrance attended the University of Arkansas where he received a Master's in Business Administration. He started his career at the Dallas office of Arthur Andersen as an auditor and later accepted a position in Atlanta, GA in Arthur Andersen's Transactions Advisory Services (M&A). After leaving Andersen in 2002, Terrance accepted a position as a Financial Controller for a business within the Emerson Retail Solutions Division ("ERS") which is a Division of Emerson Commercial & Residential Solutions. He was later promoted to Director of Finance, Director of Operations and Director of Strategic Planning. Terrance currently serves as the Vice President, Finance for ERS where he oversees all aspects of Finance and Accounting for the Division. Terrance has been married for 13 years to his wife Kerri. They live in the Atlanta metro area and together, they have two boys, Jackson (9) and Xavier (7). He enjoys playing golf, watching various sports and spending time with family and friends.

Anthony Lewis, Ph.D

Dr. Anthony Lewis is from Talladega, Alabama born to Diann L. Turner and the late Donald Jim Swain. He is married to Tiffany, and they are the proud parents of six children (Jasmine, Akirah, Anthony II, Sierra, Kailey, and Braxton). He received a B.S. and a M.Ed. in Special Education from Alabama State University as well as a Masters in Educational Leadership. He received a Ph.D. in Educational Leadership and Policy Analysis from the University of Missouri. Dr. Lewis began his work career as a special education teacher at Jefferson Davis High School (Montgomery, AL), where he taught for six years. He was later appointed Assistant Principal then Principal of E. D. Nixon Elementary School (Montgomery, AL). Because of his successes as Principal, he was heavily recruited to work with Kansas City Public Schools (Kansas City, MO) where he currently work as Director of Elementary Schools in the Department of School Leadership. In this position, Dr. Lewis provides leadership for elementary principals, schools, and programs; oversee school planning, implementation, coordination and evaluation of elementary schools and ensure that program activities comply with District policies and Missouri Statutes. Dr. Lewis is also a Certified Facilitator for the National Institute for School Leadership (NISL).

Herman Moncrief, CPA

Herman Moncrief is originally from Prattville, Alabama, and currently resides in Spring Hill, Tennessee. He is married to April and is the proud parent of fraternal twins, Asia and Bryce. He received a B.S. degree from Alabama State University, with a concentration in accounting in 1997 and is a certified public accountant in Georgia.

Shortly after graduation Mr. Moncrief relocated to Atlanta, Georgia, and began his professional career as a staff accountant for The Maxim Group. Mr. Moncrief subsequently has served as staff and senior auditor for Arthur Andersen, corporate controller for InterCept, Inc., audit manager for KPMG, LLP in Atlanta, Georgia, and corporate controller and principal accounting officer of American Software, Inc. (NASDAQ:AMSWA). American Software is a publicly traded software company operating primarily in the Enterprise Resource Planning (ERP) and Supply Chain segments of the software industry.

Mr. Moncrief currently serves as the vice president of finance for MEDHOST, Inc. Mr. Moncrief is responsible for all aspects of accounting and financial reporting, in addition to managing and directing the general accounting, billing, credit, collections, and tax functions of the company. He also serves on the boards of Turning Dreams Into Realties (TDI) and the United Way of Williamson County.

Jeremy Spratling

Jeremy L. Spratling was born and raised in Talladega, Alabama. He graduated from Auburn University at Montgomery with a bachelor of science degree in economics in 1996. He graduated from the Graduate School of Banking at Louisiana State University in 2007. He worked in the financial services industry for 14 years before founding Corporate Facilities Management, Inc. Mr. Spratling handles the day-to-day operations and management of Corporate Facilities Management.

He is married to Freddie, and they have an active daughter and a son. He enjoys fishing, reading, and physical activity and community involvement. Mr. Spratling mentors youth, business owners, and aspiring entrepreneurs.

Demetrice Jones

Demetrice A. Jones attended Alabama State University (ASU) in 1993 and earned his bachelor of science degree in criminal justice. In 2003, he enrolled in the ASU graduate program and received his master of science degree in general counseling. Demetrice is CEO of Clear Path Youth and Family Services, LLC, which is located in Montgomery, Alabama. His agency provides counseling services for at-risk youths who encountered personal, family, and behavioral issues at home, in their communities, and at school.

Demetrice also serves on the management team at a local financial institution. Demetrice has also written and published two relationship novels, *When the Truth Is Revealed* (2008) and *If He Won't, I Will* (2009). He is currently working on his third novel, *Now That the Truth Is Revealed*.

ABOUT TDI

In the fall of 1993, a group of over ten young men from Talladega, Alabama, and Dallas, Texas, met as freshmen on the campus of Alabama State University. They started what is now a life-long friendship with a common ambition to be successful and a desire to use their knowledge, time, and monetary gifts to give back through an organization they founded called TallaDallas, now operating as TDI.

MISSION STATEMENT

TDI's Mission is dedicated to assisting people to turn their dreams into reality by providing scholarships, mentoring, and professional development. Through our story and brand, we will help by developing or enhancing leadership qualities, equipping people with tools for professional growth, or coaching habits for success.

VISION STATEMENT

Our vision is to advance human well-being by assisting in developing holistic, well-rounded individuals who will become positive contributors to society and will in turn assist in reciprocating that effort for future generations of young men and women.

UNIQUE FEATURES

Collectively, the members of TDI have over 100 years of experience in a variety of disciplines such as:

Accounting

Management

Administration

Sales

Community Development

Criminal Justice

Education

Public Relations

Publishing

Ministry

Music and Entertainment

Human Resources

Advertising

Entrepreneurship

Organization Initiatives

Scholarship Award Program

Mentorship Program

Professional Development Seminars and Workshops

Internship Program

Community Service and Outreach Program

Career Camp

SUPPORT OUR MISSION

Book our DREAMS Professional Development Seminar for your next event, tailored to motivate and inspire professionals to achieve their dreams.

Consider partnering with us by making a tax-deductible contribution. Your donation will go toward the awarding of collegiate scholarships for the upcoming school year.

By making a donation to TDI, Transforming Dreams Into Realties, you will be entitled to a unique opportunity to participate in our programs. Depending on the level of your tax-deductible donation, you will be entitled to some of the following benefits:

- Recognition on all scholarship and mentorship promotional materials/media (fliers, posters, and press releases).
- Recognition at our planned events to individuals in attendance to include but not limited to annual scholarship fundraiser and our professional development seminars held on the campuses of institutions of higher learning at various times throughout the year.
- Opportunity to introduce and briefly speak about your products or services at our events.
- Opportunity to set up an exhibit booth at events.

If you are interested in being a partner of our organization, please make checks payable to TDI, Turning Dreams Into Realities, and send donations to PO Box 270933, Flower Mound, TX 75027-0933. Or you can donate through our secure online PayPal account at www.tdi2r.org.

Should you need additional information, do not hesitate to e-mail us at info@tdi2r.org. Thank you in advance for your support.

Connect With TDI

TDI
PO Box 270933
Flower Mound, TX 75027-0933

E-mail
info@tdi2r.org

Website: www.tdi2r.org
Facebook: www.tdi2r.org
Twitter: @turningdreams

CPSIA information can be obtained
at www.ICGtesting.com
Printed in the USA
FFOW03n0858130418
46211375-47532FF